THE 49ERS
Super Champs Of Pro Football

BY LOU SAHADI

QUILL

New York   1982

Library of Congress Catalog Card Number: 82-50250

ISBN: 0-688-01309-0 (pbk.)

Printed in the United States of America

First Quill Edition

1 2 3 4 5 6 7 8 9 10

Writing a major work under excruciating time pressure could never have been possible without the editorial tenacity of Bruce Lee and Kristina Lindbergh, to both of whom I am deeply grateful, and the art design of Gerry Repp. Special thanks also to George Heddleston of the San Francisco 49ers, Lou Anne Smith and Eric Daum who were of great help from the beginning.

Cover Photo by Mickey Palmer
Inside color photography and black and white photographs by Michael Zagaris and Dennis Desprois.

CONTENTS

To Ed DeBartolo, Jr. who had vision; Bill Walsh who had genius and Chico Norman who had patience for 27 years. Finally, to Morris and Christopher who would never go across the Bay to see an Oakland game.

Lou Spadia was there when
the 49ers began in 1946.

THE EARLY YEARS

Lou Spadia was with the 49ers in the beginning and it hadn't been all that good. Now, 35 years later, Spadia could enjoy what was happening. He remembers what it had been like in the early days of the All-American Conference, when, besides the tough times and lean years, they had had winning teams and even played in two championship games. Sitting in his office as the director of the Bay Area Sports Hall of Fame, the pleasant, mild-mannered 62-year-old Spadia represents a patriarchal link to the early days of professional football in San Francisco.

"The similarity then and now is so damn striking," Spadia began. "I look at little Eddie DeBartolo, Jr. now and I see Tony Morabito in his 30s. And take Bill Walsh. Damned if you don't see Buck Shaw's silver hair. Not only do they look alike, but they seem to have the same kind of approach to their players, the same pixyish sense of humor. Neither one takes themselves too seriously. Neither one considers himself a demigod."

Tony Morabito, who started the 49ers back in 1946, didn't get off on the right foot in his hometown. He was a friendly individual, and was passionate about his team, but he managed to incur the wrath of the San Francisco Chronicle the very first year. Looking for newspaper support, he had agreed to play an opening exhibition game for five years for charities sponsored by a rival newspaper, the San Francisco Examiner. When that contract expired, Morabito prudently, or so he thought, decided not to renew the agreement. That made the Examiner upset. And since the Chronicle never forgave him for what he did initially with the Examiner, the 49ers were left without strong newspaper support. Nothing could have been more damaging to the club's struggle for fan interest, especially when college football was so popular in the Bay Area.

Still, Spadia had some precious memories of those early years. He had been the first front office member hired by Morabito, so he had done everything: answer the phone, write letters and work as the ticket manager. During pre-season games that first year, he even performed as the equipment manager. Another of his endless responsibilities was to make travel arrangements for the team. It wasn't as easy as it sounded. Operating on a survival plan, Spadia transported the players on two planes. Fearful of a crash, the coach would give Spadia the passenger lists for each plane, carefully splitting the players by position. Quarterback Frankie Albert would have to be on one plane and the team's reserve quarterback, Jesse Freitas, on the other. Running back Norm Standlee was put on a different plane from running back Joe Perry, until everyone down the line was meticulously accounted for.

On long trips to the midwest and the east, the team would be away from San Francisco for weeks at a time. Spadia would then have to arrange for two busses to transport the players. One bus became known as the "good apple" and the other as the "bad apple"—for obvious reasons.

"The bad apple bus would stop and pick up three or four cases of beer, bread and salami," Spadia said. "The good apple bus would always arrive about two hours before the bad apple bus. One quarterback was always on the bad apple and one on the good apple."

In 1957, Tony Morabito died of a heart attack at age 47, during the halftime of the Chicago Bears—49er game he was attending at Kezar Stadium. The Bears were leading 17-7 at the time. When news of Morabito's death reached the players in the dressing room, they responded with a furious second half rally that beat Chicago, 21-17. After the game, one of the Bears spoke to Albert, who was now the 49ers' coach.

"If he was going to die, it would have made him happy knowing you beat us by four points," the Bear said.

"To have him alive, it would have made me happy to lose by a hundred points," Albert replied, breaking into tears.

Spadia has more fond memories of Morabito, many that others have never shared.

"Tony was an extraordinarily friendly man," says Spadia. "He'd hitch rides on garbage trucks to go to fine restaurants. He knew everybody. But he was always throwing things. One day Gordy Soltau sauntered into the office wearing a hat. Gordy was still playing, but he was starting out in business then. Those were the days when businessmen always wore hats. Tony wouldn't have it. He let out a shriek, grabbed that hat and flipped it out the window. Now, our offices in those days were

2

Quarterback John Brodie was one of the greatest in San Francisco history.

Quarterback Y.A. Tittle teamed with receiver R.C. Owens to thrill 49er fans with the "Alley Oop" pass.

10 floors up, so we all rushed over to the window to see what had happened to the hat. Well, it fluttered down right at the feet of some poor guy standing on the sidewalk below. He looked up as if he was expecting a body to follow."

In 1957, Spadia became the 49ers' business manager. The next year, he went to College Station, Texas to sign Charlie Krueger, a star tackle at Texas A&M, who was the 49ers' number-one draft choice and later played 15 years for the 49ers.

"I figured the guy's too skinny," Spadia recalled after Krueger agreed to sign. "I asked him to sign but Krueger refused to put his name on paper. He said, 'Sir, I can't do that. My team still has to play in the Gator Bowl.' It's always best to get a player's signature as soon as you agree to terms. I guess it's like a car salesman. He promised me he would sign after the Hula Bowl. For the next three weeks I called Charlie every other night, and he would say, 'Sir, I gave you my word.' It's just that I kept having nightmares of this Cana-

Running back Hugh McElhenny was known as "The King."

Another outstanding 49er quarterback was Frankie Albert, left, who later coached the team, above, when his playing days were over.

dian guy putting down a thousand dollar bill and Charlie going for it and ending up in the Canadian League."

Meanwhile, death seemed to hover over Kezar Stadium. In 1964, Tony's brother, Vic, died. The ownership passed to the widows of both brothers, Josephine and Jane. They made Spadia president and general manager in 1965.

The following year, Spadia suffered more contract traumas when quarterback John Brodie threatened to jump leagues and sign with the Houston Oilers in the rival American Football League for a reported sum of a million dollars.

"It destroyed my son's college graduation for me," Spadia said. "I was at the commencement exercises but couldn't keep my mind on what the guy up there was talking about, with our quarterback in Houston. Fortunately, Brodie was the only football player I knew, or know of, who didn't allow money to interfere with his attitude toward the game or

Tackle Leo Nomellini, who played both ways, was another popular player.

7

his performance. When we got him a defense, he showed people how good a quarterback he was."

The 49ers won their first Western Conference championship in 1957, three years before the American Football League began. The Niners had an exciting club featuring the famous "Alley Oop" pass from Y.A. Tittle to wide receiver R.C. Owens. The play accounted for a number of last-minute victories. The maneuver was solely dependent on the leaping ability of Owens, a former college basketball star. Tittle would lob a high pass in front of the goal post and Owens would time his leap and outjump the defenders.

That's not to say that the 49ers were a one-dimensional team that year. Far from it. Some of the greatest stars in the team's history played then, including halfback Hugh "The King" McElhenny; fullback Joe "The Jet" Perry; tackle Leo Nomellini, who played both

ways; wide receiver Billy Wilson; defensive back Dick Moegle; tackle Bob St. Clair and kicker Gordy Soltau. San Francisco fans not only remember their old heroes but the NFL championship they lost when they blew a 27-7 lead to lose to the Detroit Lions, 31-27. San Francisco fans were stunned.

There were other championship hopes after that, all of which ended in frustration. In three successive years under Coach Dick Nolan—1970, 1971 and 1972—the 49ers missed a trip to the Super Bowl. The most painful experience was in '72 when San Francisco was ahead of Dallas, 28-16, with only 1:53 left in the first playoff game. However, in that brief period of time, the Cowboys scored, recovered an onside kick and won the game on the second of Roger Staubach's touchdown passes.

"I felt so sorry for those guys when the game was over that I couldn't even look them in the eye," said Dallas guard Blaine Nye.

Brodie, being chased by Los Angeles' Merlin Olsen, played 17 years with San Francisco.

"With five minutes to go, I didn't think any of us believed we had a chance to win."

The game was a personal defeat for San Francisco's wide receiver Preston Riley. He is remembered by every 49er fan as the one who muffed Toni Fritsch's onside kick, which was recovered by defensive back Mel Renfro at midfield, and set up the Cowboys' winning touchdown.

"It was a hell of a kick," said Riley. "I think it hit me on the right shoulder pad. It just took a funny bounce. I thought I had it. Of course, it bothered me a lot back then. But I didn't dwell on it a whole lot because I still thought I might be playing for a few more years. I felt like I had just gotten to be a pretty good receiver. Of course, I wasn't All-Pro or anything, but I had started about half the time I was with San Francisco. I felt like I was really coming into my own. I don't really think that much about it anymore, though. I still like to remember the good things and not dwell on that too much."

Brodie, who was the quarterback then, sympathized with Riley. He felt he was blamed excessively when the 49ers cut him before the 1973 season.

"Preston Riley was made the goat for something that wasn't his fault," Brodie said. "It

Tony Morabito   Vic Morabito

Jane Morabito, left, and Josephine Morabito.

was one of the rankest tricks I've ever seen in pro football, and the blame goes right to the top—the coaches. They all of a sudden started playing scared, like they were afraid to lose a game. Nobody says anything about the 55-yard drive Dallas put together against our defense or the 50-yard drive to win. Riley never said anything to anybody about it and didn't bellyache. He was too big to get into an argument. It was a shame he had to go out that way."

Five years later the old 49ers changed hands. The Morabito family sold the team to Ed DeBartolo, Jr. in 1977 and it marked the beginning of a new regime, one that would bring San Francisco to its first world championship.

Defensive tackle Charlie Kreuger played 15 years with the 49ers.

9

ED DeBARTOLO JR.

For Ed DeBartolo, Jr., the memories of what happened when he bought the San Francisco 49ers in 1977 are not pleasant. He paid $17 million for the franchise and what he got the next two years were heartaches. During that period, the entire organization was in chaos. The 49ers were losers on the field and fan dissent was heard throughout the city. Losing is a disheartening way of life, and the blame quite naturally goes right to the top. When the guy at the top is young and handsome and a relative stranger to San Francisco and the world of professional football, it's easy to pass the blame off on him. Ed DeBartolo, Jr. knew the feeling all too well—the feeling of being the new kid in town.

One of the first things he did his first year as the 30-year-old owner of the franchise was to fire Monte Clark, the 49ers' head coach. He took that bold step after the popular Clark had led the Niners to an 8-6 record in his first year the season before. That wasn't such a significant record except that it happened to have been the 49ers' first winning campaign in four years. That one winning season gave Bay area fans hope of seeing a championship for the first time.

"Does everyone fully realize that we made an investment of $17 million?" DeBartolo asked at the time. "This is a business, not a playtoy. We're not going to placate personalities."

The young owner's remarks weren't viewed kindly by the local press. (Clark was friendly with the media.) However, DeBartolo was trying to reorganize the 49ers, and he entrusted the job to Joe Thomas, who had earned a reputation with two expansion teams (the Minnesota Vikings and the Miami Dolphins) for being a sound judge of player talent. It didn't take long for DeBartolo to realize that Thomas' way of doing things wasn't going to work. The Niners reverted to their losing ways with a 5-9 record the first season. Then coach Ken Meyer was fired and Thomas brought in Pete McCulley, who had remained loyal to him at Baltimore during a coaching insurrection. McCulley didn't last a season. He was replaced by Fred O'Connor after the ninth game of a 2-14 season in 1978 that made O.J. Simpson wonder why he'd ever come back home to finish his career in San Francisco.

DeBartolo couldn't wait for the season to end. Frustrated 49er fans grew physical. At one game he was hit on the head with a beer can thrown from the stands. It made him

Former all-time great O.J. Simpson, right, makes a point with DeBartolo as Ronnie Lott, left, looks on.

wonder.

"I couldn't believe someone would throw a full, unopened beer at me," DeBartolo jokes. "The least the guy could have done was drink it first."

DeBartolo knew that the two years under Thomas were a mistake. What was even more important, he admitted his miscalculation in public. By that time, naturally, Thomas had become nervous. Even the players felt the tension and it was clearly reflected in their play. Certainly, no club owner ever had a rockier beginning.

"You take a licking, but you have to keep ticking," says DeBartolo. "Joe Thomas had become an island unto himself. You can't become an island when you're in the entertainment business. You can never be bigger than what you're trying to do. He couldn't take the gas. It wasn't easy for any of us. If I was going to be in Youngstown, Ohio and still be the owner of a San Francisco team, then I had to have somebody very visible who would be able to take the heat.

"At the last, Joe was communicating with no one. He wasn't talking to the media, and he wasn't talking to me. What concerned me as much as our record is the fact that our image and status in the community had suffered. Our family has always been in the people business, and that means doing things in a first class manner, being fair and cooperating as much as possible with the public and the media.

"Being an owner is a support function. If an owner doesn't have the brains to hire good people and then stay out of the action himself, then he has no business being in sports."

The next decision was DeBartolo's and his alone. He wouldn't listen to any of the people around the league who were advocating a new coach and a general manager. The coach he wanted was in his backyard. All he had to do was convince Bill Walsh at Stanford University that he should return to the National Football League, this time as a head coach. Like DeBartolo, Walsh had been frustrated by professional football, though for a good deal longer. DeBartolo's decision turned out to be sound.

"When we needed somebody to take com-

DeBartolo checks out a practice session with his vice president of personnel John McVay.

mand of the team, Bill Walsh was the first and only person I talked to," DeBartolo says. "He had been at Stanford for two years, so I had heard a lot about him in the Bay area, and when I met him, I felt he had everything I wanted in a coach and a general manager. He was intense and intelligent. He had composure and was his own man.

"The future of pro football rests in having your coach out-coach the other team's coach. It's such a sophisticated game now that you need an offensive genius with defensive knowledge, someone who's not only able to adjust to what the other team is doing, but who is also able to readjust after the other team adjusts. To me, Bill Walsh is at least five years ahead of his time. He's a difficult man to know deeply.

He's very open when interviewed. He's likeable, serious and intelligent, but he's an extremely private man. The day we met was a lucky day for both of us."

The DeBartolo-Walsh union showed decisive results by the second year. When DeBartolo went ahead and made Walsh general manager as well as head coach, the chemistry worked. DeBartolo gave support from the management level and Walsh concentrated on the field operation. Walsh couldn't have been happier on his return to pro football.

"Ed's extremely enthusiastic, extremely loyal," says Walsh. "He's never questioned our staff's discretion in financial matters. Owners like a certain kind of person. It's not specifically profiled, but they need to trust the

The young owner has the highest admiration for coach Bill Walsh.

people who work for them because they have given such autonomy. He knows about football and he's learning more. But one of the fortunate things is that he knows it's a rather diverse business and you can't dabble in it and be successful. So he doesn't dabble."

DeBartolo wouldn't dabble in *any* business enterprise. When he and his father purchased the 49ers from the Morabito family they looked on it as an investment. Ed, Jr. already had a solid background with the family's corporation at its headquarters in Youngstown, Ohio. It was a multi-million dollar shopping-mall-investment concern that had had a most inauspicious beginning.

Back in World War II, Ed DeBartolo, Sr. relieved the boredom of his stint with the Army by engaging in frequent dice games. He won more than his share of pots and wisely sent his winnings home to his wife, Marie. The gambling earnings began to add up. Ultimately, they formed his grubstake. In 1949, Eddie, Sr. erected the first shopping mall in Youngstown. That was only the beginning. Today the DeBartolo Corporation lists 47 shopping centers, with more on the planning board.

What's more, the company's assets are no longer restricted to shopping centers. Its corporate web now encompasses two banks, three race tracks, hotels and motels, an overseas shipping terminal and free port, the Pittsburgh Penguins hockey team, industrial and executive office parks, and the Civic

DeBartolo shares a moment of joy with running back Paul Hofer.

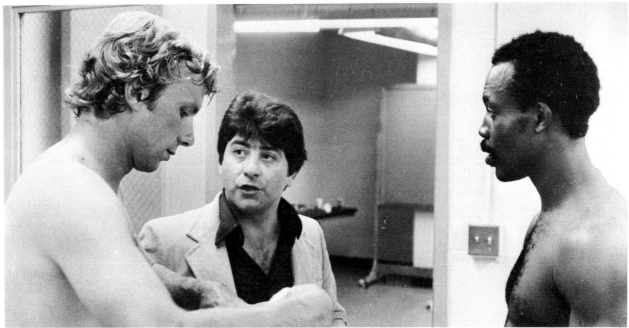

In a somber mood, DeBartolo talks to quarterback Joe Montana and receiver Fred Solomon.

Arena in Pittsburgh. Although still energetic, DeBartolo, Sr. has turned over the operation of the family empire to his only son, who functions as president and chief executive officer. The two are close. Ed. Jr. has a great appreciation for what his father has accomplished.

"When he got out of the Army, my father had about $5,000, and he invested it in two duplexes," he says. "His first shopping center was a three-store strip center in Youngstown. My father and I spend a tremendous amount of time together. He's really become more like my brother. We have coffee every morning at six.

"We develop from concept to completion. Then we manage and operate. We never sell anything. Everything is 100% owned by us. We design everything ourselves. We look at everything as a total entity. We're concerned not with what we've done but what we are going to do next. Our philosophy is to keep moving, keep building."

DeBartolo has a demanding workload—one that finds him spending many hours aboard the company jet. He often works a six or seven day week. Yet the family remains close. A great many Saturday nights are reserved for dinner at home where Eddie is often the chef, operating the barbecue in both winter and summer.

"My spare ribs are the very best in that part of the state," he often boasts, adding, "our close friends are the ones we went to school with. We've known some of them for 20 years. They're nice people except for one thing. On a cold winter night, some of them cook in their garage. The only place you can really do ribs right is outdoors."

He also remains close to the 49ers. Though he doesn't interfere with his coach, during any given week he'll make several phone calls to Walsh. It's just DeBartolo's way of keeping in contact. DeBartolo's call to Walsh several days before the team's championship title game against the Dallas Cowboys is a typical example.

"We talked about Ronnie Lott's great game against the Giants," says DeBartolo. "I asked him about the weather, and I asked him if there was anything I could do. It was the only time we talked that week and Bill was very friendly—gave me a lot of time. We don't like to interfere with our executives, but we like to keep in touch."

Through it all—the fame, the success—DeBartolo remains a low key personality.

"When the 49ers were available, I contacted the Morabito ladies and made the deal," said the elder DeBartolo. "Then I turned the club over to Eddie and he's done it."

DeBartolo and Walsh walk arm and arm after a victory.

BILL WALSH

He's a refreshing personality. He's different. There is no harshness in his voice. There are no explosive outbursts; no temper tantrums. He is not an advocate of strict discipline in a sport that seems to worship at that shrine. Rather, he approaches his work scientifically, like a professor in a chemistry laboratory. In many ways, he personifies the college professor—his neat white hair, his preppy clothes, his crisp, well phrased explanations. There isn't another coach in the National Football League who draws more X's and O's on a chalkboard than Bill Walsh.

In his short, three-year tenure as head coach and general manager of the 49ers, Walsh has established a reputation for genius. Certainly his accomplishments during that period support this thinking. In his first year with the 49ers, in 1979, San Francisco finished with a 2-14 record. The following season they improved noticeably, to 6-8. In 1981 they reached the summit. Not only did they finish with the best record in the NFL, 13-3, they didn't stop until they'd vanquished Cincinnati, 26-21, in Super Bowl XVI. No coach in the history of the game had ever achieved so much in such a short time.

It hadn't been all that easy for Walsh. He began his coaching apprenticeship at Oakland, his first job in the NFL, in 1966. The year he spent as assistant backfield coach under Al Davis was a valuable training ground. Davis was an innovator and a master of offensive football. Walsh learned well. Concentrating on the passing game, he learned how Davis burned opponents with the long pass and an element of surprise. He also noted how Davis refined the short and medium passing attack. Then, during his next eight years at Cincinnati, Walsh applied that knowledge and began to win recognition as a brilliant offensive coordinator. His talent for developing quarterbacks was formidable. Under Walsh's tutelage, Greg Cook became Rookie of the Year in 1969, leading the league in passing. In 1974 and 1975, Ken Anderson won two passing titles, the only quarterback in history to win the award in back-to-back years.

Yet inexplicably, Walsh could not get a head coaching job. When Paul Brown finally retired as coach of the Bengals in 1975, staying on with the team as general manager and vice-president, Walsh was passed over for Bill Johnson. At that time Walsh was a strong candidate for other vacancies as well—with the

New York Jets and the Houston Oilers. But the one spot he had really expected and had in fact waited for, was Brown's job. It was Walsh's first major disappointment. He was so disillusioned and frustrated that he began to look seriously at some of the other jobs. Brown didn't appreciate it at all. A fiercely proud individual who demanded loyalty, Brown viewed his offensive coordinator's intentions as an affront. Anyone who knows Brown well knows that he never forgives or forgets such breaches. Essentially, nobody quits Paul Brown. And though Walsh is too much of a gentleman to say that he'd been blackballed, that seems to many to have been the case.

Word soon leaked out that Brown had told Walsh he would never be a head coach in the NFL. As Bob Trumpy, who played for Brown and the Bengals for ten years and is now a successful television network sportscaster says, "Once you're off Paul Brown's Christmas card list you never get back on. First of all, Bill Johnson was a helluva guy. But Paul also knew that Johnson was not going to change the ballclub. It was going to stay in Paul Brown's image. Walsh was different. He had to argue for everything, even the smallest changes in offense, like putting a tight end in motion.

"Walsh's intent was to make the defense work; make them make a tackle. When we passed, he wanted completions. He didn't want the ball on the ground or out of bounds. We all begged him not to go, but he said he couldn't afford to wait. He had to go where he had a chance to be a head coach."

The logical place in 1976 was the New York Jets, and there were insiders who felt that Walsh would replace Charlie Winner, who had been fired. It never happened.

"I was one of the two finalists for the Jets' job; the other was Lou Holtz, of course," Walsh said. "What hurt my chances for the Jets' job, I believe, was the Jets figuring—how could I be a very good coach if Paul Brown had passed me over when he needed a head coach? I had aspirations for the Bengals' job; I had hopes. But there was no bitterness toward Tiger Johnson, who was a very competent coach and a very good friend of mine. No bitterness on my part at all, only vast disappointment."

Walsh has a word for the defense.

Rebuffed, Walsh made a lateral move to San Diego where he served as offensive coordinator for the Chargers' 1976 season. In that one year, he transformed Dan Fouts from an all but unranked passer to one of the best in the league. Walsh then went to Stanford University for the 1977 season as head coach. He immediately turned the Cardinals' football program around and got Stanford into bowl games in both 1977 and 1978. He also helped groom a number of quarterbacks for the pros: Guy Benjamin, Steven Dils and Turk Schonert.

"At Stanford, he was a breath of fresh air," says Benjamin. "He treated players like adults and gave us more responsibility. Traditional football coaches seem to baby athletes—look after them. They make sure they go to class and are in bed by 11. They take them to a movie and give them ice cream. With Bill, instead of pointing around and telling you what to do every time, he shows you once and expects you to understand it. He allows you to surround yourself with an air of responsibility instead of an air of dependence. I think that is one reason his players perform so intelligently

on the field.

"Bill handles you in a way that makes you think he is handling a business matter that just happens to be football. The same approach would probably be successful in some other business. Bill realizes that different people have different thresholds, emotionally and intellectually, and he tries to account for that. He gets close, but not too close. He gets funny, but not too funny. He can get you up, but not uptight. And he can keep you loose, but not lose you.

"He could be tough; he could be tough with the best of them. The good thing was that he never let it get boring. Pro scouts would come to the practices and they'd wind up copying down our plays and formations and taking them back with them to the NFL."

After one season at Stanford, when the Cardinals finished 9-3 (including a Sun Bowl victory over LSU), Walsh was a leading candidate for head coach of the Los Angeles Rams. Instead, the job went to George Allen who then didn't even last long enough to start the 1978 regular season. Allen was the choice of Carroll Rosenbloom, the Rams' owner, who

The tension is evident on the faces of Walsh and his players just before the kickoff.

had ignored the advice of his son, Steve.

"My father's strongest consideration was that he just had open heart surgery, and he was beginning to think about death for the first time," young Rosenbloom recalls. "He began to feel the frustrations of getting into the playoffs for so many years and then failing to win the Super Bowl. I heard my father say many times, 'I'd rather not get into the playoffs than to get this far and lose.'

"If he was looking for a long-range coach at the time, Bill Walsh would have been the prime choice. Bill was seriously considered. But then Allen, who had been with Washington, became available. All of a sudden, Bill Walsh became a moot issue. Bill Walsh had made a very good impression on all of us. My father seemed excited about Bill. We could see with Bill Walsh a long term situation, which is what we always sought. But the whole attitude changed when George came on the scene. God knows what would have happened

if George hadn't surfaced. It would have come down to Bill Walsh and Ray Malavasi. My father was impressed with Bill Walsh."

The fact that he didn't get the Los Angeles coaching spot just deepened Walsh's beliefs that he would never get such a position in the NFL. Paul Brown's wrath still hung over him.

"Personally, I was rather close to getting the job, maybe closer than the public was aware," says Walsh. "But there was a concerted effort to stop me. In certain circles I was undermined and it worked. But I must admit I was educated as to the tactics and extent some people would go to professionally. The money was tremendously attractive, I must admit, and I honestly feel I was the only candidate at one point. But taking my family and my obligation to Stanford into consideration, I can't say that I would have accepted the Rams' job in the final analysis."

A year later, Walsh didn't hesitate to accept the 49ers' offer. Maybe because it was an

open, honest offer, without the chicanery that he had come to expect from the fellowship of the NFL. San Francisco owner Ed DeBartolo approached Walsh just nine days after Stanford produced one of the greatest comebacks in the school's history: it overcame a 22-0 halftime deficit to defeat Georgia in the Bluebonnet Bowl, 25-22. Displaying his confidence in Walsh's ability to lift the 49ers up from defeat, DeBartolo gave his new coach the title of general manager three weeks later. Walsh now had full control of the football operation and of San Francisco's fortunes.

Two years later, on the day he left for San Francisco, Walsh recalled his first day at Stanford when he gathered all his assistant coaches together for a get-acquainted meeting. He leaned back in his chair and unexpectedly tumbled over, which immediately broke the ice. The day he chose to tell them he was going to San Francisco, he called them together again. The very same thing happened, only

this time, by design. He leaned back and rolled out of his chair. He wanted to go out the same way he'd come in.

"I did sort of get lost in the circle of the NFL," Walsh said. "I came into pro ball because I thought I would thrive on the technical part of the NFL. Then I saw men whom I had worked with becoming head coaches, and I was still an assistant. That was one of the most frustrating periods. When I got to San Francisco it was so choatic that I was very fortunate. Anything I did would have been an improvement. I could have said, 'Okay, everybody in that room,' and that would have been a good start."

Walsh did a lot more than that. He turned to the college draft as his prime resource and selected two prospective stars—quarterback Joe Montana on the third round and wide receiver Dwight Clark on the tenth round. He also looked at hundreds of free agents because he didn't have a number-one draft pick that year. It was in the free agent market that Walsh reaped a harvest. He signed defensive end Dwaine Board, running back Lenvil Elliott, safety Dwight Hicks and tight end Eason Ramson.

Still, it took time for the Niners to show a significant improvement under Walsh. After a 2-14 record in 1979, Walsh added even more new players to his system. They included such draft choices as running back Earl Cooper, defensive end Jim Stuckey, linebackers Keena Turner, Craig Puki and Bobby Leopold, and punter Jim Miller. He also added two excellent free agents in running back Ricky Patton and defensive end Lawrence Pillers, and traded for tight end Charle Young from the Los Angeles Rams. There was a marked improvement as San Francisco finished the 1980 season 6-10.

Walsh's biggest windfall came in the 1981 draft. He stunned the pro-football establishment by drafting three defensive backs out of the four selections he had in the first three rounds. They were cornerbacks Ronnie Lott and Eric Wright and safety Carlton Williamson. All became starters. Walsh also profited once again in the free agent area, signing such notable players as linebacker Jack Reynolds, running backs Walt Easley and Bill Ring, and wide receivers Mike Wilson and Mike Shuman. Trades added running backs Amos Lawrence and Johnny Davis, defensive end Fred Dean, tackle Dan Audick and Quarterback Guy Benjamin.

Surprisingly, Walsh himself never played professional football. His career as a coach began in the mid-1950s at San Jose under Bob Bronzan, for whom he played as an end for two years. Walsh has the greatest admiration for his teacher.

"Bob Bronzan was a man ahead of his time," says Walsh. "He was a great theorist, a highly detailed football coach. He coached it as a science, a skilled sport. Dick Vermeil was a junior there when I was a graduate assistant. People ask me how well I knew Dick at that time. Well, I can assure you we found each other very quickly. We were very close. I have to smile sometimes when I hear someone comparing his work habits to mine—when he's called a workaholic, while I work more or less normal hours. That's just Dick. He was always

Walsh made cornerback Ronnie Lott his number one draft choice in 1981.

like that in everything. Tremendous industry and drive, like no one else I'd ever seen.

"It's a sad fact that in the NFL, the way Dick works makes some people nervous. What is your typical NFL club, anyway? At the top you've got an owner who made it quick, who wants things to be done quickly on his club without knowing how. Under him, you've got the general manager, who's positioned himself firmly within the owner's comfort zone. He demands a large salary for doing very little. Then you've got a personnel man, often a frustrated player or coach, who justifies his position by sending scouts out.

"Then there's the coach, in there with his assistants at night, looking over the films again and again, trying to find out what's wrong. And at the same time, there are the owner and general manager and personnel man out having dinner, discussing the team over their third martini. The general manager says, 'Well, I don't know what's wrong. Look, I've got the best facilities and administration and exhibition schedule. I've set up every possibility to do a job.' And the personnel man says 'We've got the players. I had a great draft. I know because I read it in the papers; but everyone knows Smith is a guard, not a tackle. And the general manager says, 'Everyone knows so-and-so should be playing, and everyone knows so-and-so should be the quarterback.' And then they say, 'What do we do?'

"So they put their heads together; and they get a new coach, obviously within the general manager's comfort zone, not too strong a threat, a guy who knows where he got his job from. So the cycle starts all over again and the situation continues to exist. Why? The big money that is made—TV, NFL Films, the hype. Football should get the hype. It's a great sport. Sometimes, though, well, sometimes the way teams are run makes you wonder."

Walsh was talking about himself. He had nearly been beaten by the system. During all the years he labored as an assistant within the system, he was recognized as an offensive virtuoso. Yet he could never get a head coaching job. When he failed to break into the system he withdrew to college coaching, but when DeBartolo reached out for him two years later, Walsh held his own. He stood alone, and the young owner of the 49ers knew it. No general manager patronized Walsh.

He was equal to the challenge. The 49ers were a team in turmoil with very little talent. That he succeeded in putting the 49ers' house in order in so short a time is a tribute to his abilities as an organizer, to his judgment and to his keen understanding of player psychology. He established his priorities and fulfilled them, leading San Francisco to a world championship within three years.

"The reason for our success, the reason for the turnaround, is because of three things," Walsh explains. "One: everyone in our organization has a role, no one is more important than anyone else. Two: we have an excellent coaching staff. And three: we have put together a chemistry out here where the most important thing is that I am the general manager and coach, and I get the players I want. It is my team.

"When I was asked two years ago about the team, I said we'd be a contender in two years. I don't think there was any luck involved. It was design. People ask me now if I'm surprised. Well, if you told me we were going to be 13-3, I'd say that's mighty impressive, but not surprising.

"What we've done here is to gain maturity. Over our first two years here, our drafted players are now ready to play in the NFL. We were woeful in pass coverage over the past two years, so we went out and got Lott, Williamson and Wright.

"Yet, execution is the key to our success. For instance, we depend more on our guards to block than our backs. I've developed a system of football that has been unique. Obviously, I've had success with my offensive formulations and the development of quarterbacks. I think I'm as expert as anyone coaching football today, plus I may have the artistic ability that adds a certain flair to what I do."

When Walsh was preparing to play the Houston Oilers for the first time in the 1981 season, the game was still almost 24 hours away, but Walsh already had determined what he was going to do on the opening series of downs. That's how far ahead he thinks and why he is always doodling with X's and O's at all hours of the day.

"Our first play will be a screen pass to the fullback," Walsh says, looking at a slip of paper. "Then we'll throw wide to the fullback, then we'll run dives on our third and fourth plays, knock 'em off the ball, surprise 'em, and then we'll come back to Earl Cooper on a quick pitch. Then we'll change formations on them and run our fullback in motion, strong side, and run quick-hitting patterns against the zone. We'll run Dwight Clark on an end-around on about the 12th play, and then we'll go deep to Freddie Solomon out of the slot formation."

A voice interrupts.

"Suppose everything doesn't go exactly as planned?"

"Things never go as planned," Walsh replied, "but sooner or later we'll come back to everything that's down here. Listing the offense like this makes me feel more secure, and it makes my quarterback feel more secure. What I'm hoping is that as seasons pass, people will *not* want to come to San Francisco to play the 49ers."

JOE MONTANA

He stood leaning against the wall of his locker. His hair was slightly disheveled. A few drops of perspiration still glistened on his forehead. He should have been sweaty and excited. After all, he had just thrown the most important pass in the history of the San Francisco 49ers. But he was calm, controlled. The assemblage of media with their microphones and tape recorders and notebooks didn't ruffle him. It was almost as if they weren't there. He could be alone in a crowd. That's his way—polite and shy. He answered questions effortlessly, without emotion, never once seeming upset about answering the same questions again and again for the swarm of reporters that had crowded all around him. Of all the plays in the 49ers' 36-year history, Joe Montana's pass—this pass—will be remembered.

Some five minutes before, on the soft surface of Candlestick Park, the fate of San Francisco's glorious season was in his hands. With only seconds left to play, the 49ers were trailing Dallas 27-21. The Cowboys had been there before, dozens of times, and they had always won the close games—the big ones. Now San Francisco was trying to capture the 1981 National Football Conference championship

from them. With a scant 58 seconds on the stadium clock, Montana conferred with coach Bill Walsh in front of the 49er bench. The play Walsh wanted was a spring right option. It was a pass play that Montana, possession receiver Dwight Clark and speed receiver Fred Solomon had worked time and time again in practice all year long. The primary receiver on the play was Solomon, who lines up on the inside of Clark in the slot. If Solomon isn't open on the pattern, then Montana looks for Clark.

Now the Cowboys were fighting for their lives. It was up to their defense to win the game. They braced for the attack. Montana took the snap and started rolling to his right. Three Cowboys were in pursuit and, for an agonizing moment, it looked as if Montana would be caught. He kept scrambling for time. Solomon was covered. Montana was waiting for Clark to squirm free. At the last possible second, as he fell to the ground, Montana threw into the right corner of the end zone and broke his fall with his arms. All he could hear from his prone position was the roar of the crowd. He hadn't seen that, with split second precision, Clark had jumped higher than he'd ever done to catch the pass that gave the

49ers a 28-27 victory and a trip to Super Bowl XVI.

It wasn't until after the game that Montana actually saw the 'miracle' pass on a television replay in the dressing room. It brought back memories of the Alley Oop pass that 49er quarterback Y.A. Tittle had worked with receiver R.C. Owens two decades earlier, which had accounted for numerous victories.

"I was going to take the sack," Montana explained so many times afterwards. "I couldn't see Dwight open. I knew he had to be at the back of the end zone. I let the ball go. I got hit and wound up on my back. I rolled over. I saw Dwight's feet hit the ground. I heard the crowd screaming."

Montana's role with Notre Dame was basically as a reserve who came off the bench to pull out several dramatic last-minute victories for the Irish.

A record crowd was there on that beautiful January day to see that amazing performance. Before this century is over, there will, no doubt, be many more who will claim to have been in Candlestick that day. Big plays have a way of becoming legendary, and there is certainly no bigger play to be found in the colorful pages of 49er lore. That one play also served to convince thousands of skeptics that Montana was, indeed, a superior quarterback, a high-caliber field general resourceful enough to execute game-winning passes even when throwing off the wrong foot. The Cowboys, so confident the preceding week, were stupified.

"You just beat America's team," snapped Dallas defensive end Too Tall Jones after the game.

"Well," Montana answered, "now you can watch the Super Bowl on television with the rest of America."

Montana had captured the hearts of America with that one gutsy play. At that moment every kid in the country wanted to be Joe Montana. Yet quiet, unassuming Montana, with the cherubic good looks of a choir boy, rebuffs such fame. He's almost too self-effacing to grasp the magnitude of what it means to be a superstar.

"I can't picture my name up there with George Gipp," says Montana, when asked how it feels to be a legend. "Every afternoon I muck out two horses' stalls. Do legends do things like that?"

Perhaps not. But what Montana accomplished in his first full year as the 49er quarterback—not unlike what he achieved in a somewhat sporadic career at Notre Dame—challenges the imagination. Not that it has been easy for him. In college he emerged as a gridiron hero for his ability to lead the Fighting Irish to victory with some of the most furious comebacks in the history of Notre Dame football. The curious thing was that he did so coming off the bench. It wasn't until midway through his junior year that he was given the starting job as quarterback.

Ironically, Montana had almost decided to attend North Carolina State on a basketball scholarship. He played both sports in high school in Monongahela, Pennsylvania, and ac-

Montana looks over the Chicago Bears' defense.

tually preferred basketball. However, when Notre Dame offered him a football scholarship, his father, Joe, Sr., wasted no time in extolling the glories of Irish gridiron history to him. Unfortunately, for Joe the glory had to wait. Reporting to South Bend his first year, Montana was listed as the seventh string quarterback. He was at the bottom. In his quiet way, he tried to rationalize it all.

"I am affected by things but I don't show it," Montana said. "I'm emotional, but nobody knows it. At Notre Dame I was awed by the place in general, and lonely at being away from home for the first time. There were all those other quarterbacks. I was feeling all the things people say I don't feel."

Apparently Notre Dame coach Dan Devine didn't think Montana could make it as the regular quarterback. He preferred Rick Slager. Joe still sat on the bench his sophomore year, in 1975. Tight end Ken MacAfee, who was then the team's leading receiver, and

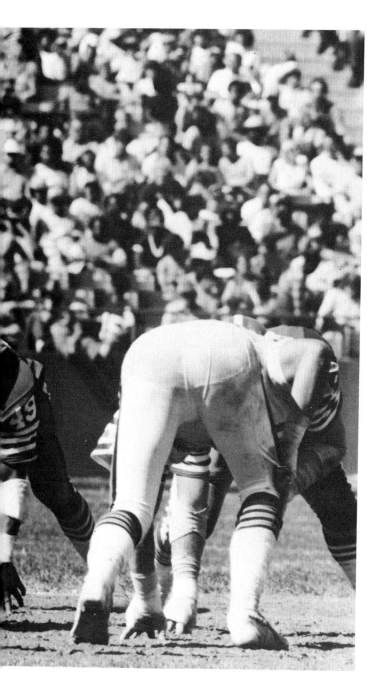

But in five plays, Montana led Notre Dame to a touchdown. He then passed for a two-point conversion to tie the game at 14-14. Even then he wasn't finished. The next time the Irish got the ball, Montana threw an 80-yard touchdown bomb that ultimately provided Notre Dame with a 21-14 victory. The young quarterback played a total of 62 seconds, yet he completed three of four passes for 129 yards. The legend was only beginning.

Then, as fate would have it, Montana suffered a bone chip in his finger during the Navy game a month later and was sidelined for the rest of the campaign—missing the final three games. He didn't play at all the following year, 1976, because of a shoulder separation. When he was finally ready to play again his junior year in 1977 (Montana was at Notre Dame five years and graduated with a degree in marketing), he found himself listed as the third string quarterback behind Rusty Lisch and Gary Forystek. If Montana was disappointed, he didn't show it.

By the third game of the 1977 season, Montana again proved he was a winner. Notre Dame had been having its troubles. Though they won their opening game as expected, they were then upset by Mississippi. Against Purdue, it looked as if the Irish were headed for their second defeat. Lisch wasn't doing too well and was finally yanked late in the third period with the Irish behind, 24-10. In came Forystek. He only lasted one play before he was hit so hard that he was removed from the game on a stretcher.

Montana thought he would get the call, but to his surprise, Lisch returned to the field. Montana's hopes sank. Once again, Lisch proved to be ineffective, and with a minute left in the quarter, Devine turned to Montana. As Montana ran onto the field to join the huddle, his teammates on the bench started jumping up and down. They were cheering for a third string quarterback. That's how much confidence they had in Montana.

"It was the most amazing sight I've seen in 30 years of attending football games," said Roger Valdiserri, Notre Dame's assistant athletic director. "The team thought Joe would pull it out, and, of course, he did."

He did, although the way he started raised

later played for the 49ers, couldn't figure out why Montana wasn't the number-one quarterback his first two years.

"The pattern began to be that Slager would start the game and then Montana would have to come in and save it," he said.

That pattern first took shape in Montana's sophomore season in a game against North Carolina when Montana finally got a chance to play in the fourth quarter. The Tar Heels were on the verge of upsetting the Irish, 14-6.

I WILL NOT BE OUT HIT
ANY TIME THIS SEASON

some eyebrows. The first play he called was a sideline pass, which sailed into the stands. When the team returned to the huddle they looked somewhat apprehensive. Montana noticed it.

"Don't worry about that," he told them. "I was a little nervous. I'm okay now. Let's score some points."

Score they did. In the final quarter, Notre Dame scored 21 points under Montana, to pull out a 31-24 victory. Montana had completed nine of 14 passes for 154 yards. Strangely, Devine still preferred to start his other two quarterbacks ahead of Montana.

A week later Montana took on the Air Force Academy. The scene was familiar. Entering the last quarter, Notre Dame was behind, 30-10. Montana came on and sparked the Irish to a 31-30 victory. Later that season the Irish were behind the University of Pittsburgh, 17-7, when Montana appeared on the field for the first time with just 10 minutes left in the game. There in front of his home-town fans, he pulled out a 26-17 triumph. By the season's end, Montana's dramatic finishes helped earn Notre Dame the national championship.

Montana's success continued into his final year at South Bend, though not without some disappointing moments. In one game Notre Dame was playing against a strong rival, the University of Southern California in Los Angeles before a large crowd. At halftime the Trojans were in command with a 17-3 lead. Montana then led the Irish on to a 25-24 lead only to be victimized by a last minute field goal, and his team lost, 27-25.

He saved the best for last. To maintain their high ranking in the polls, Notre Dame had to defeat the University of Houston in the 1979 Cotton Bowl. That New Year's Day certainly wasn't made for football. The temperature in Dallas was 17 degrees and 30 mile-an-hour winds buffeted the old Cotton Bowl. Montana didn't feel well. He was bothered by the wind and cold and had cuts on his hands from the rock salt, which had been spread on the field to melt the ice that formed during the night. When he wasn't on-field, Montana hunched over the portable heaters to keep warm.

The Irish were behind at halftime. But Montana's condition was even more alarming. He couldn't stop shaking. A doctor took his temperature and discovered that it had fallen

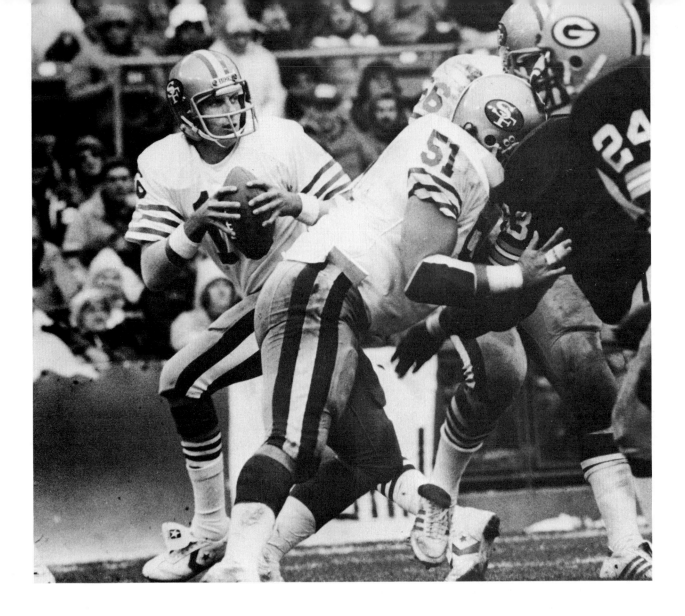

below normal, to 96 degrees. He was quickly wrapped in blankets and given several cups of chicken soup in an effort to raise his temperature. But by then, Notre Dame had fallen further behind. They were trailing Houston, 34-12, with time running out in the third quarter.

Then the Montana magic surfaced. Defying the cold and bitter winds, he led the Irish to a dramatic 35-34 victory, with a touchdown pass at the very end and no time remaining on the clock. The winning pass was a direct result of a miscue on the previous play. There were only four seconds left when Montana threw what could have been a touchdown pass to Kris Haines. However, Haines slipped and the ball fell to the ground.

"We went back into the huddle with two seconds to go and Joe said, 'Don't worry, you can do it,' " Haines recalls. "He gave me that little half-smile of his and called the exact same play, right on the money for a touchdown."

"In a way, I was fortunate," says Montana. "I was lucky to be in a spot where there was a lot of pressure, what with it being Notre Dame, a place with a great quarterback tradition. The comebacks, they just happen that way. They're not something you plan on. I guess I'm just lucky in those situations. I don't know, I guess I get excited when something like that happens. You have to be in games like that. You try not to let it get to you, but in some situations when the game suddenly has things going your way, you have to get excited. You have to."

Despite his triumphs the pros weren't waiting with open arms for Montana. Scouts considered his arm suspect. They also felt he was frail at 6'2" and 185 pounds. None of those who had observed him during his final season at Notre Dame considered him to be a blue chip prospect (the status reserved for college players who are selected in the first two rounds of the college draft).

"I wasn't too worried about the draft," says Montana. "I knew wherever I went I would have to prove myself. I've always had to prove myself."

None of the scouting reports made an impression on Walsh. He doesn't hold scouting opinions as sacred and has always had his own judgments on players or prospects. While everybody else turned their backs on Montana as a pro prospect, Walsh selected him on the third round of the 1979 draft.

"The scouts have no command of what the quarterback position takes, but they are good at reinforcing each other's opinion at what they don't know," he says.

"All they care about is how tall he is, his build, how heavy he is, his delivery, and if he can throw the ball a country mile. They said Montana was erratic, skittery, not particularly well built, not particularly strong-armed, and he had a side arm delivery.

"I can't find any negatives about his arm. Maybe the so-called experts can. People who say it's only an average arm are mistaken. And they always will be. Because his delivery is not a flick of the wrist like Terry Bradshaw's, they think it's not strong. He throws on the run while avoiding a pass rush, and he does not have to be totally set. He is not a moving platform like some others who are mechanical and can only do well when everything is just right. Joe performs well under stress. He's a natural football player, really a natural competitor. He competes instinctively. It's like he's so used to competing that he's not in awe of it or of himself."

Walsh had a direct influence in developing Montana. And it turned out to be the perfect teacher-pupil relationship—Montana, a raw, undeveloped talent and Walsh, a virtuoso in producing the consumate quarterback. Walsh started at the beginning, as if he were teaching a baby to walk. In the first eleven games of his rookie season, Montana threw only two passes.

In the twelfth, a week later against the Denver Broncos, he recorded the first touchdown of his pro career. The first pro game he ever started took place two weeks later against the St. Louis Cardinals.

"Early in Joe's second year, I privately decided he was to be our quarterback," says Walsh. "As a rookie on a poor team, he did a fair job in all. But his skills were obvious. He was just so active, so quick on his feet, so instinctive. The second year we eased him in so as not to break him."

Montana started 1980, his second season, as a reserve quarterback behind Steve DeBerg. He had spent the first year learning the system. Now, under Walsh's timetable, he was scheduled to play more. Still, up until his first start, Montana had thrown only six passes that season. They all came in one game against the New York Jets in New York, which the 49ers won, 32-27.

DeBerg started the game with a bad case of laryngitis. It was so bad that DeBerg was wired with a special microphone in order for his teammates to hear his signals. With San Francisco on the Jets' five yard line, DeBerg called a timeout and ran to the sidelines, supposedly for repairs on his microphone. The timeout turned out to be subterfuge. Walsh had planned it all the way. He sent in Montana, who immediately carried out Walsh's instructions and effortlessly bootlegged the ball on the very first play for a touchdown, and, before the game was over, tossed two touchdown passes to Dwight Clark.

Then in mid-October, Montana started three straight games, only to find himself back on the bench after that. He didn't get another starting assignment until a month later.

The game everyone remembers best was against New Orleans, the first week in December, when Montana authored the greatest comeback in the history of the NFL. Halfway through the game, the 49ers were behind the Saints, 35-7. When the second half began, Montana replaced DeBerg and steered the 49ers to four touchdowns that tied the game at 35-35 and sent the struggle into overtime. He kept right on in the overtime, directing the Niners on a 55-yard march that resulted in a game-winning field goal, 38-35. Montana had

completed 24 of 36 passes for 285 yards and two touchdowns, and ran for a third touchdown himself.

"You get in that situation and people tend to get excited," says Montana. "Some people become afraid, afraid they're going to make a mistake. I'm not that way. I just kind of like being in those situations. I don't look forward to it, but I can handle them. Maybe it's just because it's more of a challenge than any other time. I don't exactly relish the pressure, but I don't fear it. I think it is just competitiveness that makes me that way."

Montana compiled some impressive statistics for his half-season of work. He completed 176 of 273 passes, which included 15 touchdowns and only nine interceptions. His passing percentage of 64.5 was not only the best in the NFL that year, but also established a club record. Yet, at times during the season, he appeared unsteady—not quite sure of himself. Despite the fact that he and DeBerg were essentially competing for the number-one spot, and that a two-quarterback situation can have a damaging effect on the performances of both, they were close. As roommates on the road, they shared a great deal of time together, often competing in backgammon,

cards, pitching soda cans in a waste basket or playing the electronic games for hours at a time in hotel recreation rooms.

"We could never quit because somebody was always behind," says Montana. "At practice, if one of us threw a pass that wobbled, the other would quack like a duck. We teased each other into staying friends, but we knew one eventually had to go if the other was ever going to have complete confidence. We had to play pretty cautious. As soon as you made a mistake, you looked at the sideline to see if the other guy was still standing next to Bill Walsh, or if he was warming up."

Walsh was well aware that DeBerg was the one who had to go. But it would have been disastrous if Montana had had to shoulder the load that very first year in 1979, when the 49ers finished 2-14, with inferior personnel and the recent introduction of Walsh's new system. By increasing Montana's playing time throughout 1980, he gained the necessary experience for a full season behind the center. The Niners were on their way back, having improved to 6-10 that year, and DeBerg was on his way to Denver before the 1981 campaign began.

"I was trying to set the stage," says Walsh.

"It wasn't for me to go public with my thoughts. I was preparing Joe to be our starting quarterback, so I put him in certain situations or against certain teams to give him a taste of success. Steve could see that. Then I'd pull him back. It was a three-year project.

"I don't advocate the discipline of a Marine drill sergeant. What I try to emphasize is the discipline you'll see in a ballerina or a concert pianist. Joe is like a great writer or a musician. The great asset has a counterpoint to it. Sometimes, he would wait too long and throw a bad pass. I suppose the so-called experts call that inconsistent instead of saying, 'Look at that marvelous ability. If we can only channel it.'"

With DeBerg gone, Montana was handed the ball and expected to lead the 49ers for the 1981 season. It was the first time he'd ever been given so much responsibility. In college he'd always been competing for the top spot. Now it was his. Walsh felt he was ready. However, the 49ers didn't get off to a good start and Montana gave the skeptics, especially those who questioned the DeBerg trade, reason to gloat. Montana was sacked five times in the opening-season 24-19 loss to Detroit. After defeating the Chicago Bears, 28-17, the 49ers lost to Atlanta, 34-17. San Francisco was 1-2, after three weeks, but Montana wasn't worried.

"I didn't have any doubts about the team or myself," Montana said after the first game. "A guy won't go 101 yards very often, especially when the ball gets picked off in the middle of the field. It was just a misread by myself to the tight end. I was expecting to do one thing and he did it a different way. The sacks? Well, Detroit has a very good team."

By the middle of the season, though, the 49ers themselves had turned into a very good team. They were winning week after week—though they still hadn't earned the respect that goes with winning. Montana's star quality wasn't fully appreciated until he rallied the 49ers against Dallas in those closing minutes of the NFC championship game.

It seemed that Montana and the young Niners grew together as part of the learning process that goes with winning. "I think the coming together was, first, a matter of our offensive line controlling the line of scrimmage," says Montana. "When you control the line of scrimmage, you're going to control the football. I got a lot of time to throw and the receivers did an excellent job of getting open. They've improved from last year in their pattern-reading and reading the defenses."

It had to begin with Montana, though. He had to establish himself as the unquestioned leader of the team. DeBerg had been the more vocal of the two. Montana was, in most cases, reticent, and he had to win their respect, not with words but with results. In his own unassuming way, Montana earned his teammates' confidence.

In one early season game, his two wide receivers, Freddie Solomon and Dwight Clark, were running deep pass routes. The play was designed with Clark as the primary receiver. However, Solomon got open and began to shout, "Joe, Joe." Unresponsive, Montana threw instead to a third receiver. He waited for Solomon to return to the huddle and looked straight at him.

"Don't ever yell my name again, and I'll tell you why later," he snapped. Montana didn't want Solomon distracting his concentration out loud.

It was probably the harshest statement he ever made to a teammate, but in doing so he had established his position. By the end of the NFC championship game, he had confirmed his status. Many of the Cowboys didn't have much respect for the 49ers. And Too Tall Jones was a bit more vocal than some of his teammates. He was quoted as saying that he didn't respect the 49ers even though they had soundly beaten Dallas, 45-14, several months before.

Montana remembered the remark and waited for the right moment to retaliate. It came during the second quarter of the game when Montana faded back to pass and Jones applied pressure. Reacting instinctively, Montana faked a run, side-stepped Jones and fired a 38-yard completion to Clark. Then he turned to Jones and yelled, "Respect that!"

"On the field we're a family," he explained afterward. "When someone says something about one of my teammates, it upsets me more than if he said it about me. Jones said he didn't respect us."

Montana learned about respect as a child, growing up in Monongahela, a rural blue collar town about 30 miles up-river from Pittsburgh. Despite the fact that the town was in western Pennsylvania, quite close to the University of Pittsburgh and to Penn State, it is a hotbed for Notre Dame football fans. Notre Dame football games blared over the radio in the Montana household every Saturday afternoon. While Joe was still a baby, his father had visions of his son attending Notre Dame one day. Why not? After all, that section of Pennsylvania had produced such quarterback luminaries as George Blanda, Johnny Unitas and Joe Namath, none of whom had gone to Notre Dame. Why couldn't Joe Montana, Jr. as a Fighting Irish quarterback, be the first?

"Joe never had a chance to go to Pittsburgh or any other university," Joe Sr, admitted. "He was brainwashed. Sometimes you look at a kid and you know he's a natural. I'd come home at lunchtime and he'd have a ball and bat in his hands, standing there waiting for me when I came in the door."

By the time he was four years old, young Joe was throwing a football. His mother, Theresa, has fond memories of her son in those young years, all of them centered around sports. It was baseball in the summer, football in the fall, and basketball in the winter. When his father wasn't home, Joe would ask anyone to play catch with him. Joe and his father had a close relationship, and the elder Montana was determined that his son should succeed as an athlete. Since Joe was an only child, his father's ambition for his success was almost an obsession. He wouldn't let anything stand in the way of his son's development. All of Joe's energies were focused on sports.

"Working is for adults," his father would say. "A kid should be a kid."

So, Joe participated in sports practically all year long. He had a lot of encouragement from both parents.

"I went to all the games but one," said his mother. "It was a midget game in bad weather down the river, and the question was whether to take two cars or one. I told them one car is safer; I'll stay home.

"Joey came home with a hole in the forehead of his helmet. I was so frightened I said never again. I'll never miss another game. We went out the next morning and bought him a new helmet, one of those one-size, water-and-air helmets. He wore it through midget football, through junior high football, and all the way through high school football. I don't know if it helped him, but it helped me. I felt a lot better."

When Joe was ten years old there was a time when he seemed to tire of sports. He wanted to quit midget football. His father was upset and couldn't understand why but his mother felt that if her son didn't want to play, he shouldn't have to. She was willing to let Joe give it up. His father finally agreed, but later changed his mind.

"I said, the hell with it, go ahead and quit. After work when I got home, I said 'Get your equipment; you're going to practice. One day, Joey, things are going to get tough in your life and you're going to want to quit. I don't believe in that.'"

Several years later, when Montana was in junior high school, there was another crisis. Feeling that he should earn some money, Montana got a job as a caddy at the country club just outside of town. His father did not approve of this at all but reluctantly allowed him to do it. That is until one Wednesday night, when Montana was scheduled to pitch at a six o'clock Little League game. Montana's mother remembers it as if it was yesterday.

"When Joey wasn't there at 5:45, Joe went after him. He picked up Joey's baseball uniform at home, drove out to the country club, took him off the golf course, had him change clothes in the car, and got him to the ballpark in time for the first pitch. That night, Joey's father had a few words for him. He told him, 'We'll have no more of this, son. If you need money, I'll give it to you. If I can't afford it, you'll go without. You came close to letting your team down tonight—your team, their parents, your parents, your coach, and most of all, yourself.'"

It was incidents like these and the fact that he was nurtured by a determined father with a strong sense of values, that forged Montana's personality. He's steady, unflappable, and prefers the quiet countryside to the bright

A relaxed Montana shares a few laughs with a couple of small fans.

lights of the city. In a business where fame can be overwhelming, especially for those who make it young, he is refreshing, a little boy beneath it all.

"I want to see some things I've only seen in books," he said to his wife Cass one day. So they planned a photo safari to Kenya.

His wife understands him well. "He's curious, full of wonderment," she says. "He's not at all worldly. Joe will sit for hours and get lost in an animal book."

His love for animals goes beyond the pages of a book. The Montanas own two miniature dachshunds and two Arabian horses. The barn sits beside their house on a one-acre knoll 30 miles to the south of San Francisco, with a panoramic view of the countryside and the Pacific Ocean. "Right out our backyard there are six miles of trails down to the ocean at Half Moon Bay," says Cass.

"He doesn't ride during football season. Working with the horses is the way he lets off steam. At least I think it is. He certainly doesn't do it any other way. I know it sounds incredible, but he's always as calm as he is out on the field.

"The man I know isn't a ranter or a raver; he's not even a talker. He's very proud of his successes, but he doesn't care about fame or fortune. He really doesn't. He's very easy to live with. I'm the maniac. I liven him up, he calms me down. Joe doesn't say a lot, but whatever he does say is interesting, thoughtful. He's funny; he makes me laugh. I sometimes think that if he played football the way he conducts his life, well, he just wouldn't be a football player. He's not a leader. 'What makes you so different out there?' I've asked him. He stutters and stammers around and says, 'I don't know.' "

THE OFFENSE

The heart and soul of Walsh's coaching philosophy is organization. That's where it all begins. It is reflected in his offensive strategy. Although the 49ers throw the ball a good portion of the time, they do not do so with a high degree of risk. Rather, Walsh's strategem dictates a great deal of movement and high percentage passes that narrow the interception factor considerably. They key ingredient in achieving this effectively is a disciplined quarterback. Walsh discovered that Joe Montana had the temperament to control such an offense, and when the 1980 season ended, Walsh decided that Montana would begin the 1981 season as his quarterback. He was so certain in his judgment of the still inexperienced Montana that he traded Steve DeBerg to Denver before the 1981 campaign even began. What Walsh's teaching techniques could achieve amazed everyone, including John Ralston, a former head coach at Denver who worked several years under Walsh in San Francisco.

"Bill has done things with the offense that nobody thought could be done," Ralston said. "He puts in a new game plan every week. We coaches have always thought you have to drill players over and over before they could do anything, but Bill has run through things two or three times and expected players to do it right in a game. And they have. Once in a while you see Joe Montana call a time out because he's not sure exactly what formation they're supposed to be in. By and large, they've run the offense as well as anybody could.

"The other thing Bill has done is anticipated what defense the other team will be in and call the play to beat it. For instance, he'll anticipate that the defense will be a 'five under zone'. He'll call for a guard to pull out as if they're running a screen. The defensive backs see that and stay in tight, and a receiver like Dwight Clark will just slip through that first line of defense and be wide open. If the other team comes out in a man-to-man, he'll run picks and again a receiver will be open somewhere. I'm just amazed at the way he can anticipate."

Walsh's greatest decision, of course, was in going all out with Montana as his quarterback. It was a monumental choice since the 49ers were a young team that would be in the hands of a quarterback who had barely a half-season of professional playing time behind him. The hole card was that Montana had two extremely talented wide receivers in Fred Solomon and

Quarterback coach Sam Wyche.

Special teams coach Milt Jackson gives kicker
Ray Wersching some encouragement.

Dwight Clark.

Solomon was one of the older veterans, despite his being only 29 years old. After being acquired from the Miami Dolphins in 1978, Solomon put together two good years in 1979 and 1980 despite his being hampered at times by nagging injuries. Although he isn't big—5'11" and 185 pounds—Solomon is a deep threat receiver. He caught 57 passes in 1979 and 48 in 1980, scoring seven touchdowns each year.

"In 1979, Freddie had his best season as a pro." Walsh said. "In 1980 he was even better. He should be a vital part of the 49ers' offense for a number of years to come. I feel he has matured."

Solomon did indeed get better. In 1981, he caught 59 passes for 969 yards and eight touchdowns, all career highs. He also led the Niners in punt returns with 29. That is what Solomon is capable of doing. But his maturing had been delayed by the ragged transition he made when he joined the Miami Dolphins as a rookie in 1975.

As a quarterback at the University of Tampa, Solomon established all sorts of records, including 50 touchdowns, 39 of them running and 11 passing. He might have been one of the greatest running quarterbacks ever. In 17 games, he rushed for 100 yards or more. However, when Miami took him on the second round of the 1975 draft, they did so solely with the purpose of using him as a wide receiver. It was disappointing for Solomon.

"I had this boyhood dream of playing quarterback," Solomon said. "I liked Miami and Don Shula and everything and everybody else there. But deep down, I couldn't accept being a receiver. That dream of playing quarterback in the pros stunted my growth. I know that now."

But Solomon had to give it a try before that lingering desire was finally removed.

"They put me in to play quarterback in the last quarter of our last game in Detroit," Solomon recalled. "And then the childhood dream went away. I guess I knew all along that I wasn't cut out to be a pro quarterback. I lived my fantasy and got it out of my system. After that, I put it aside and worked at being the best receiver I knew how. What I have found

Running back coach Billie Matthews and offensive line coach Bobb McKittrick diagram strategy.

out is that all great players are consistent. I haven't been. I'm working towards that goal."

It wasn't easy. When the Dolphins traded him he found it disheartening. San Francisco acquired him along with Vern Roberson and two draft choices, for running back Delvin Williams, who had been a 1,000 yard runner and had led the 49ers in rushing for three straight seasons. Many experts felt that the 49ers had been taken. Their comments didn't make Solomon feel any better.

"It was like, 'We don't want you any more,'" Solomon said. "It caught me by surprise."

Solomon would like to forget his first season with San Francisco in 1978. He caught 31 pas-

ses, which topped everyone else, but it was the passes that he didn't catch that haunted him. He was looked upon as a classic pass dropper. On the final day of the season in St. Louis, his malady worsened. He caught one pass for eight yards, but dropped five others, two of which would have been certain touchdowns.

"It wasn't pleasant, but I wasn't dismayed," Solomon recalled. "I had knee problems, and in that game I was hurting so bad that I wanted to ask the coach to take me out. But as an athlete and a starter, I couldn't. Now, I know that I should have."

When Walsh arrived in San Francisco in 1979 not only did Solomon's outlook brighten,

Solomon with a sensational over the shoulder reception.

but he also began to blossom as a receiver. Despite the fact that the 49ers were only 2-12 in Walsh's first season, Solomon had his best year even though he suffered a shoulder separation. It was just the beginning.

"Bill taught me a lot of things about pass receiving, especially my routes," Solomon said. "I'd have to say Walsh made the difference. He doesn't yell at you but has a way of getting his point across so that you don't forget. I used to improvise, but now I realize that if I'm where I'm supposed to be, Joe can throw it up there and I can go get it.

"Joe's a lot like Bob Griese. He throws an easy ball that goes right to the receiver 90 percent of the time. Joe's smart, too—makes few mistakes. He's a lot smarter than young quarterbacks are supposed to be. He's a quiet leader. He throws the ball as good as anyone in pro football. Joe can throw the ball while drifting to the left, as good as if he simply dropped back. He is strictly a business quarterback."

And Solomon is looked upon as a big dividend receiver. He likes it, too.

"I've heard the talk about me making the big play," Solomon said. "I hope I'm looked upon that way. I just try to do my job each week and be as consistent as possible."

When the 49ers met New Orleans for the first time early in the 1981 season, the offense was lethargic the first half. In the dressing room, with the game tied 7-7, Solomon was told that they needed a big play to spark them. The coaches diagrammed it on the blackboard and they identified it as "flanker go". They told Solomon to be ready for it, that they would call the play early in the third period. On the second play, Solomon got the word. Montana hit him with a 25-yard pass and Solomon did the rest. He faked his defender and ran 35 more yards for the touchdown to snap the deadlock and boost the team's spirits.

Besides catching, Solomon takes pride in his blocking. Most wide receivers aren't concerned about that aspect of play, but Solomon works on it. It has paid off. He is considered one of the better blocking receivers in the game.

"We've spent a great deal of time on the

48

wide receivers blocking," Solomon said. "Obviously, it's not one of the glamorous parts of the position, but we've found it really makes a difference in the game. Beyond the fact that you never know when you might be making the last block that allows one of your backs to break a really long gain. Going after the defensive backs makes a big difference in the way you play against the pass.

"Usually, the defensive back is the aggressor. They will use that aggression to try and knock you off your game. But by attacking them, you negate that a little. All of a sudden they have this wide receiver coming after them. They get so involved about your throwing blocks at them that they begin to think more about that than covering you. A lot of people say Dwight Clark and myself are the best blocking wide receivers in the NFL today."

Clark is a contrast to Solomon. Physically, he is bigger at 6'4" and 210 pounds. When Walsh made him a number ten draft choice in 1979, everybody laughed. They did so because in his final year at Clemson, Clark caught a total of only 12 passes. Nobody wastes even a tenth round selection on someone with such paltry statistics. Certainly, none of the NFL scouts were impressed with Clark. He was regarded as nothing better than free agent material.

Although he practically went unnoticed his rookie year, Clark attracted attention in 1980.

Wide receiver Fred Solomon with a touchdown catch against Chicago.

Wide receiver Dwight Clark.

He caught an eye-popping 82 passes, which was the most by any wide receiver in 49er history. Clark accounted for 991 yards and eight touchdowns and was considered one of the bright spots in San Francisco's future.

"He is a much better football player than any of us could have anticipated," Walsh said. "He's an all-weather receiver who can catch the ball in any situation. Pro football scouting systems are imperfect systems. We miss a lot of players and Dwight's a perfect example of that. It's also true there are a lot of high draft choices who shouldn't have been drafted at all. Luck is an important element in the success or

failure of a lot of young football players coming into the NFL.

"I went to Clemson in January 1979 to look at their quarterback, Steve Fuller. We were in dire need of a quarterback then and I wanted to see him throw. I arranged to have Dwight catch for him that day in the stadium. Well, for our needs, I was more impressed with Dwight than I was with Fuller. I liked his size, speed, hands, attitude, everything about him."

Actually, Clark played in the shadow of Clemson's other wide receiver, Jerry Butler. Butler was highly regarded by the pro scouts. In fact, the Buffalo Bills selected him on the second round of the college draft that same year.

"My college career at Clemson was pretty boring," Clark laughed. "I started some games but I was really a part time player for three years. I ran in plays, too. They tried to make me a defensive back my sophomore year, and I threatened to quit, transfer to Appalachian State and play basketball. I actually put all my stuff in my car one day and I'd driven 50 miles before I thought it through and turned back.

"Really, I'm lucky. I was lucky Bill Walsh was there that day. I'm lucky he likes tall receivers and I'm lucky I had a good training camp in 1979 and made the team. I'm lucky I was taught how to block properly at Clemson. I caught a few big-play passes in games at Clemson, but none that actually won a game. In high school, I was a quarterback who couldn't pass very well."

For a time, Clark gathered more notoriety for being the boyfriend of Shawn Weatherly, Miss Universe 1980 than for his football talents. They had been college sweethearts at Clemson. Shawn was a regular jogger back then and would always try to make Clark follow the same routine, which he didn't like doing. They were a handsome couple—Shawn with her beauty and Clark with his boyish good looks. Their demanding careers have kept them apart for months at a time, yet they have an understanding about their responsibilities in the limelight.

"We are boyfriend and girlfriend just like we always have been since we went to Clemson," Clark said. "But notoriety has placed a strain on things at times. I was proud of her when she won Miss USA and Miss Universe. That was her Super Bowl."

The catch that put Clark in the spotlight also carried San Francisco into the Super Bowl. It came in the final seconds of the NFC championship game against Dallas, and it capped Clark's accomplishments for the 1981 season. He led the 49ers in receptions with 85 for 1,105 yards, surpassing his previous season's high of 82 catches.

"Dwight is most unusual," receiver coach Milt Jackson said. "He has deceptive speed, good hands, an exceptional feel for getting open and is a solid runner after the catch. He

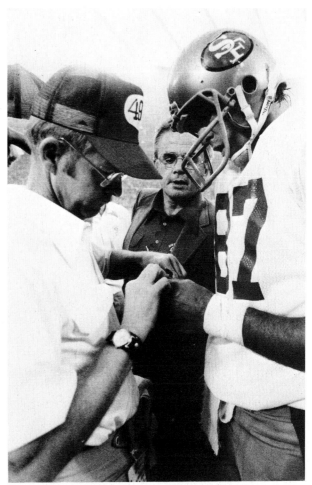

Clark gets repairs on an injured finger.

is durable and became our Mr. Clutch."

What Clark accomplished in 1981 didn't go unnoticed by Walsh—not that anything does. Walsh is careful about singling out a player for praise because he preaches a team philosophy. He couldn't help, however, saying a special word about Clark.

"It would be hard to single out one of our people after the season we've had, but Dwight is certainly a key figure," Walsh remarked. "He's the best third down receiver in the NFL. He's got great hands; he can run, he runs great patterns; he maneuvers extremely well around linebackers and he's a good blocker.

"Probably the best thing about him is his stamina. He can run 40s in 4.6 all day. There are faster receivers, but with many of them if you lined them up and had them run 40s one after the other, their speed would start to fade after the third or fourth one. With Dwight, he just doesn't lose it. He's as fast in the fourth

51

Tight end Charle Young.

dent that I need to be stronger," Clark said. "I really need to be stronger. I could be a lot better player if I were stronger. It's really bothersome to a defensive back to have somebody cutting around his legs all the time. A lot of times you're doing it to get the defensive back thinking about getting blocked instead of covering you.

"When I was in college, I always thought that if I ever got a chance to catch a lot of balls, maybe I could get into the pros. But I never did anything in college. I had a receiver coach who taught me how to cut-block. A receiver who can block has a big edge that first year in summer camp. You can be in training camp with, say, 20 receivers and maybe some are faster than you and catch the ball slightly better. But if you're the better blocker, pro coaches love that. You've got an edge."

The 49ers got another edge when they acquired tight end Charle Young from the Los Angeles Rams for a middle round draft choice in 1980. What Young did was establish leadership and experience to the young 49er line. It was somewhat symbolic since Young had languished on the bench for the three years he was with the Rams. During that time, he only caught a total of 36 passes, the longest of which was only 23 yards. Young looked at his experience philosophically, which is one of his leadership traits.

"Those Ram years were three of the most productive of my life," Young said somewhat nostalgically. "I learned patience, to persevere, to cope and to deal with problems. When a man can deal with the situation I was in with the Rams, it tells something about the man's character. Besides, playing so little for them probably added three years to my career."

His career began with Philadelphia. The Eagles made him their number one draft pick in 1973, and the former University of Southern California star made some strong statements that some people looked upon as arrogant.

"As the jet engine revolutionized air travel, so will I revolutionize the tight end position," Young said at the time.

He proceeded to do just that. In his first year he caught 55 passes, then a career high of 63. In 1975, he caught 49 and followed the

quarter as the first."

Clark isn't completely satisfied with what he's done the last two seasons. He's determined to become a stronger blocker by undertaking a weight lifting program. He has had his share of one-on-one battles with defensive backs and doesn't intend to come out second best.

"Every game I play, it becomes more evi-

Wide receiver Mike Wilson.

next year with 30. In his four years with the Eagles, he had pulled in 197 passes. But in 1977 he was traded to Los Angeles.

"I knew what I was doing the whole time," Young said of his years with Philadelphia. "I knew I was a quality product, so all I was doing was advertising. Sony advertises. General Motors advertises. What was wrong with Charle Young advertising. The way I saw it,

the average NFL playing career lasts four-and-one-half years. What was I supposed to do wait three years to make a name for myself? That way I'd only have a year and a half to cash in on it. I didn't think that made a whole lot of sense.

"So, I talked a lot. I think people misunderstood me in the beginning. They called me arrogant and braggadocious. I could tell some

Tight end Eason Ramson.

Wide receiver Mike Shumann.

of the veterans didn't like me. But I didn't care. I knew I could back up everything I said. And I did back it up. The Philadelphia fans responded to it. They liked having a guy who wasn't afraid to stand up to the Dallas Cowboys and the Minnesota Vikings.

"The Eagle image back then was suffering. I mean, the Eagle is supposed to be a big, majestic bird. Powerful wings. Sharp claws. A bird that soars to the heights. A mean ol' bird that will rip your face off if you mess with it. The Philadelphia Eagles weren't anything like that when I got there. They were more like some little, flabby chicken that was getting kicked all over the barnyard. I said, 'This isn't for me', so I set out to change it.

"And we did turn it around in 1973. Roman Gabriel, Harold Carmichael, Jerry Sisemore, Guy Morriss—we shook some people up. I look back on that year with a lot of satisfaction. In fact, I have nothing but good memories of my time in Philadelphia."

When Dick Vermeil took over the Eagles in 1976, Young's role as a big play receiver di-

minished noticeably. Advocating a ball control concept, Young had to do more blocking than pass catching. He was practically a third tackle on the field. The same thing happened to him with the Rams. In his three years in Los Angeles, he appeared mostly in short yardage situations, sitting behind the Rams' regular tight end, Terry Nelson. Young doesn't like to discuss it.

"That's a negative," Young remarked, "and I sweep all negatives into the trash can. Deep down, I knew I should be playing. But I couldn't come out and knock Terry Nelson. It would have looked like sour grapes. People would have said, 'There goes Charle Young again. He doesn't know when he's washed up.' So I just had to wait for the right opportunity. I knew I'd get another chance somewhere and I'd prove my point there."

Walsh gave him that chance and immediately put Young into the starting lineup in 1980. He quickly began to pay dividends by catching 29 passes for 325 yards. In 1981, he improved his performance with 37 catches for

Running back Lenvil Elliott.

Running back Amos Lawrence.

400 yards and five touchdowns. His 37 receptions were the most by a San Francisco tight end since Ted Kwalick in 1973.

His inspirational leadership helped the 49ers in 1981. Young was one of two 49ers who had been in a Super Bowl before. He knew what it took to get there and made it a point at an opportune time to instill the feeling in his teammates. They didn't forget.

"The night before the NFC championship game against Dallas, we had our team gathering as usual, when we watch highlight films and loosen up by entertaining each other," Randy Cross explained. "Then when it was just about over, Charle Young got up and held up his Super Bowl ring. He kind of put things back into perspective. He told us what we would be playing for—a shot at the Super

Bowl and all that goes with it. It was the kind of spontaneous talk that inspires you."

Young didn't stop there. In the closing minutes of the Dallas game, the 49ers were trailing, 27-21. There was only 4:54 left in the game and San Francisco went back into the huddle. They were deep in their own territory on the 11 yard line and needed to go 89 yards in that short span of time to pull out a victory. Young remained cool.

"There was a lot of chatter in the huddle but then Charle spoke up and said, 'Okay, let's do it,' " Cross said. "Of all the things that were said, he was the one guy I remembered and I think it was that way with most of us. When Charle says something you listen."

Apparently the players did a lot of listening to Young all season. They voted Young the

Running back Ricky Patton.

team's most inspirational player, which meant a lot to the veteran.

"This has been a great year," Young said. "It's hard to imagine one greater. When we started out, we had this tough schedule and all these rookies and everybody was saying we'd be lucky to win four games. Then we set a club record for wins, we beat Dallas twice, we won the first conference championship in 49er history and then the Super Bowl. And when that all happens, I'm voted the team's most inspirational player. That means a lot to me. Now I understand things like leadership and character and how it all fits together."

However, it didn't all fit together for Earl Cooper the early part of the season. The big running back was just short of sensational the year before as a rookie. He led the 49ers in

rushing with 720 yards and in pass receptions with 83. The name they hung on him was "Super Cooper." During one stretch on the 1981 campaign, Cooper was in a heavy slump. In seven games he gained only 31 yards, far below what was expected of him.

Cooper was puzzled by his slow start. Perhaps it was the soft turf at Candlestick Park? Was it the migraine headaches that buzzed in his head? He began to play less as Walsh began employing five and six running backs a game. It was quite a change from his rookie season, one that Cooper had to adjust to.

Walsh was concerned. He spoke to Cooper privately, trying to help the big fullback.

"You're trying too hard," Walsh said. "Just read the blocks and run. Don't make so many cuts. Get from Point A to Point B as quickly as

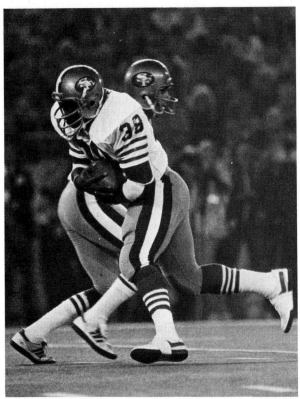
Running back John Davis.

you can."

Finally, near the end of the season, Cooper seemed to have found himself. In a 21-3 victory over the Cincinnati Bengals, Cooper enjoyed his biggest game of the season. He finished with 62 yards in 12 carries, 57 of those yards coming in the second half. He also caught six passes for 34 additional yards. He appeared ready for the 49ers' homestretch run into the playoffs.

"I don't know why I had my best game of the season today," Cooper said later in the Riverfront Stadium dressing room. "Just as I can't explain why I've played below par all season. I will admit this, the turf here sure seemed easier to cut and move on than that at Candlestick; but then a good back should be able to play anywhere.

"It has been very, very frustrating. I like to think I'm a 60-minute man like I always have been. I know I have a different running style from Walt Easley or John Davis. They are pounders and I'm just a runner. It's not a matter of strength, it's a matter of style.

"I've never had a bad year before. Being a starter has never been a question. Now I play a

few plays and sit on the bench the rest of the game. I never know when I'm going in or when I will have to sit out. It's something hard to overlook after I played every snap as a rookie."

The big, 6'2", 227 pound Cooper was San Francisco's number one draft pick in 1980. When Walsh selected him, some experts scoffed. They didn't feel Cooper was worth a number one choice. Walsh loves such criticism.

"Some of the scouting intelligentsia criticized us for taking him," Walsh said. "Earl is the finest combination runner-receiver to come up to the draft since Chuck Foreman. He has all the essentials—size, speed, hands and great athletic ability."

Walsh was so certain about Cooper that he traded the team's star runner, Wilbur Jackson, to Washington before the 1980 season ever opened. Cooper even impressed former running back star O.J. Simpson.

"He is the instinctive type of runner who will make his mark in a big way," Simpson said. "He could be another Franco Harris. Earl keeps his feet close to the ground like Franco and shifts and cuts like him and has similar size."

Harris' former running mate, Rocky Bleier, understood what Cooper went through in his second year with the 49ers. Walsh employed the multi-back system, using his runners like pawns in a chess game, with great success.

"Cooper's much better than his statistics show," Bleier said. "I know, from a player's point of view, it's difficult going in and out of a game. You lose the tempo. Plus, it's psychologically bad because if you carry only five times, your margin of error becomes very small."

Still, Cooper managed to finish the 1981 season as the Niners' second leading runner with 330 yards. He also caught 51 passes for 477 yards. The one pass everyone will remember is the one he caught in the Super Bowl, which provided San Francisco with its second touchdown and put Cincinnati in a 14-0 hole.

"Earl has a specific role in our offense," Walsh said. "He is one of the best pass-catching backs in pro football. Part of the reason we have not used him more often is

Quarterback Guy Benjamin.

Running back Walt Easley.

Running back Paul Hofer.

Running back Bill Ring.

Guard Randy Cross.

Tackle Keith Fahnhorst.

either because of defenses we faced or because game situations called for something else."

What Walsh had hoped for when the 1981 season began was to pair Cooper with Paul Hofer, the Niners' versatile halfback. Hofer had the biggest season of his five-year pro career in 1979 after having been used sparingly his first three years. In 1979, Hofer led the 49ers in rushing with 615 yards, and in pass receiving with 58 for 662 yards. However, he was sidelined after the sixth game of 1980 with a serious knee injury, so grave that his availability for the 1981 campaign was in question. Walsh was hoping but couldn't really depend on Hofer to open the season.

"If we hold Paul out in the pre-season games, say from four to six regular games, then we'd still have him for 10 to 12 contests," Walsh reasoned. "If his rehabilitation goes well, he'll still be a big factor in our offense and our season. The biggest mistake would be to bring him back too early. We won't use him until we get everyone's okay and then some. Paul is a great performer and an outstanding leader. When healthy, he is one of the outstanding backs in the NFL. He could be a 1,000 yard rusher if he could put together a full 16-game season."

It seemed that Hofer was always fighting to save his career. In 1978, his third season with the club, Joe Thomas, then the general manager, wanted to get rid of him. In his first two years, he saw only spot play as a little-used reserve. In the final pre-season game of 1978, Hofer was listed as the fourth back on the depth chart about to be cut. He got into the game against Denver late in the third quarter. His teammates knew how much the game meant to Hofer. They blocked with such intensity that Hofer ran for 120 yards and made the team. He gained 465 yards that season.

By 1979, Hofer became a starter. He responded by leading the 49ers in rushing with 615 yards and in pass receptions with 58. His

Center Fred Quillan.

Guard John Ayers.

value was in his versatility. He was the type of back Walsh looked for and needed when he took over that year. Hofer was off to another strong season in 1980 until he suffered his knee injury. The injury was so severe that all Hofer had was hope—not much more. He had to rehabilitate his knee with a vigorous off-season program and his return, even to training camp, was doubtful.

"Early in the spring I was very, very depressed," Hofer admitted. "I was used to being so active. I did a lot of running, but I couldn't do that any more."

Hofer wasn't ready mentally when he reported to training camp in July. After a couple of weeks, he had resigned himself to quitting, but his teammates talked him out of it. Hofer worked hard. He survived the final cut but when the season opened, he was still not ready physically. It wasn't until the third game, against Atlanta, that Hofer contributed offensively by catching a pass. Yet, he couldn't play

all out. He needed more time. Halfway through the season, Hofer was still struggling.

"It's frustrating day after day to see films where the linemen open up holes and I can't cut," Hofer said. "I've lost a little confidence. We had a goal line play against Pittsburgh. I was supposed to follow the guard, and if I had, I would have scored. But I saw another hole and gained only three yards. Now I grab at the first thing I get. When the linemen have a blocking combination that works perfectly and I miss the hole, I feel ashamed. When I get the ball, I know people are counting on me. I like that. If I drop the ball, I hurt the team. If I make a good play, I help it. I feel responsible."

In the next to last game of the 1981 season, Hofer's knee betrayed him a second time. He reinjured it against Houston and was out for the rest of the season. There wouldn't be any playoffs or Super Bowl for the popular runner.

61

Guard Walt Downing.

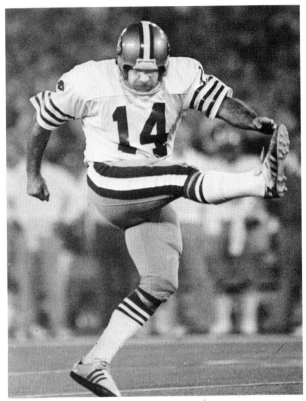

Kicker Ray Wersching.

"I felt sorry for myself for a couple of days after I got hurt in the Houston game," Hofer said. "We had already clinched a playoff spot, and I knew I wasn't going to be able to play. It's still exciting and I still feel I contributed something to help the team get this far. It wasn't much, but there were a few key plays that helped the team."

With Hofer ineffective, Walsh turned to Ricky Patton to bolster the running game. Nobody knew exactly what to expect of Patton except that Walsh had a sixth sense about him. Patton, who was cut by Atlanta after the fourth game of the 1979 season, hooked on with Green Bay only to be released midway through the 1980 season when Walsh signed him. He only carried the ball one time in the nine games in which he appeared for San Francisco. Yet Patton opened the 1981 season against Detroit and led the rushers with 72 yards on only 12 carries. He did the same thing the following week against Chicago, gaining 67 yards on 14 attempts, and scoring two touchdowns, one of them on a 31-yard pass. By then, Walsh realized he had found a replacement for Hofer.

"That was the first time since I joined the 49ers that they ever threw me a long pass, so I don't know how they thought I couldn't catch one," Patton said. "I ran my post pattern and the linebacker went so far and just stopped like he thought they would never throw deep to me. I was wide open—all alone. It was a special touchdown for my wife. She told me she was pregnant and I said I would celebrate somehow by scoring a touchdown."

Patton's performance that day had another significant meaning for him. That's because another relative, Walter Payton of the Bears, was watching from the sidelines.

"We are first cousins; our mothers are sisters." Patton explained. "I never saw him, really, until I transferred from Ferris State to Jackson State. He had just been drafted and we worked out when he came back from the Bears' mini-camp.

"He was the one who made me realize you have to play tough in football. I used to have this image of a running back gliding outside, slipping inside and sprinting down the field. He got me to be hard-nosed—taught me some tricks he learned in the mini-camp. We got to be pretty close. I owe him a lot. I probably wouldn't have made it this far if he hadn't helped me out."

Patton kept on going the rest of the season. He led the 49ers in rushing with 543 yards and added 195 more yards on 27 pass receptions.

"Our team has to use everybody," Patton said. "We use all 45 men. We pass the ball more than we run it, but I wouldn't say that's a difficult transition for a runner. You're used to running the ball and you block more here, that's all. You can pretty much tell when we're going to have a running play. Basically, it's when we're in no type of trouble. But on third down, nine times out of ten, it's going to be a pass. You adjust to that."

Patton couldn't adjust at Green Bay but he made the transition easily in San Francisco. It was a matter of coaching personalities. He didn't appreciate Packer coach Bart Starr's approach; he preferred Walsh's way of doing things. That was obvious the day that Starr took out a bullwhip at a team meeting to make a point. The symbolism wasn't appreciated by any of the team's Southern black players. Patton doesn't like to talk about it.

"It's past, and I don't care to go into it," Patton remarked. "I never said Coach Starr was a racist. Those words never came out of my mouth. To me, the kind of coach I would like to see is like Bill Walsh—loose. To me, Coach Starr wasn't loose. Bill Walsh can put the head coaching job aside and joke with the guys. Starr was the kind of guy who just walked around and didn't get involved—just walked and looked and observed.

"During practice, if he's trying to show you something, Bill Walsh might get out and run the route himself. Not that fast, but he does it. He's involved 100 percent. He knows he's the head coach and we know it, too. That lets him come around and be one of the guys, crack a joke once in a while."

Walsh also needed more help with his running game. It came in all forms—trades and free agents. Johnny Davis joined the 49ers in a trade just before the 1981 season opened. But Walt Easley, Bill Ring and Amos Lawrence were free agents. Near the end of the season, after Hofer got hurt, Lenvil Elliott was reacti-

vated from the injured reserve list.

A solid blocker, Davis provided the Niners with strong inside running, especially in short yardage situations. He was not only the team's third best runner with 297 yards, but led the 49ers in "touchdowns, rushing" with seven. Easley finished as the fourth leading runner with 224 yards while Ring added 106. Elliott contributed heavily in the NFC championship game against Dallas in the winning touchdown drive. Lawrence provided the Niners with explosive kickoff return power, averaging 25.7 yards with Ring next at 21.7. San Francisco's offensive arsenal was rounded out by reserve quarterback Guy Benjamin, a free agent, and wide receivers Mike Wilson and Mike Shumann and tight end Eason Ramson.

The other scoring weapon was kicker Ray Wersching. Although he injured himself in the season's opener and missed the next four games of the season, Wersching led the club in scoring with 81 points. He hit on 17 of 23 field goal attempts, booting all nine he tried inside the 30, and was perfect on all 30 of his extra point tries. Hampered by his injury, Wersching, for the first time in three years, failed to lead the league in accuracy.

Wersching is a dependable kicker under pressure. Since he was signed as a free agent in 1978, Wersching has kicked seven game-winning field goals for San Francisco. He topped the 1981 season with a heroic Super Bowl performance in which he booted four field goals and two extra points, accounting for 14 of the team's 26 points. What makes him so successful is his deep concentration; he never looks up at the goal posts.

"I get my bearings from the hash marks," Wersching commented. "If the stadium was in a dense fog that closed all the airports, zero visibility, it would make no difference to me. As long as I know where the hash marks are. Have you ever taken a look at the goal posts since they changed to one post and two uprights? It looks exactly like a needle. Looking into the eye of a needle—I don't need that. Which is why I never look at it once the game starts."

When the 1981 campaign began, San Francisco's offensive line was regarded as nothing more than average by the experts. Before the season ended, they had these same experts shaking their heads in disbelief at the protection they gave Montana, which enabled the team's passing game to function so effortlessly. Only 29 times all season did the opposition get to Montana, which averages out to less than two sacks a game. Putting it into perspective, Montana was sacked only once in every 20 pass attempts.

Still, the offensive team is a strange lot. None of the linemen currently play in the original position in which they began. Left tackle Keith Fahnhorst came to the 49ers as a tight end; left guard Randy Cross arrived as a center; center Fred Quillan reported as a tackle; right guard John Ayers began as a tackle, but had never played on offense; and right tackle Dan Audick was a bear wrestler. They are a product of good chemistry and hard work. Together the line totals 27 years of experience, which isn't a lot.

"We're a bunch of over-achievers," said Fahnhorst, who in his eighth year as a 49er is the veteran member of the line. "I think, talent-wise, we might not be the best athletes, but we work hard and we work together. It's tough to play offensive line here. I think we get less help from our backs and tight ends than just about anyone else in the league. We have to pick up just about anything the defense throws at us. We have real good camaraderie because we're been together for about three or four years now. It's a great unit to work with, and Bob McKittrick more than anybody else, brought us together because he has a way of handling people. I've never had a coach that's as honest as he is and as straightforward."

"Many, many times I thought I'd never see the day when I'd be on a championship team. Many times I thought about getting into some other line of work, and I wasn't sure if it would be my choice or not. It was a sick feeling going to work every day, putting out all that effort and having everything go wrong. The only thing that kept me here was that I was close to a lot of guys; I had a lot of friends. But there were a lot of times when I wanted to get out and get into a more stable situation. I could see a lot of players stuck with a losing team for a whole career. It's a shame."

Next to Fahnhorst, Cross is the oldest member of the inner line. Since they've been together longest, they developed a close friendship.

"I hate reading 'veteran offensive lineman' ", Cross said. "When I think of veteran offensive lineman, when I first got here they all chain-smoked and sat in the corner. I don't think of us that way. We've been together for four or five years and not only do we play together, we're real good friends. I've got a relationship on and off the field with Farny that's fantastic. I'm sure it wouldn't be the same if I was playing next to another guy.

"I enjoy playing guard. The difference between the two positions is that at center you can't be as aggressive. You have to call blocking signals and you're always starting with that one hand on the ball. At guard, you make more decisions on the move. I like that. Our line never got a lot of attention."

When Cross moved from center to guard in 1978, Quillan took over. He's been there ever since.

"We all complement each other very well," Quillan said. "We've been together for a number of years and that makes all the difference in the world. We know each other's habits, strengths and weaknesses. We have a way of communicating with our buddies next to us, our own little code, one word or a couple sometimes. Communicating at the last split second is vital. For instance, Keith Fahnhorst might have a safety lined up next to him and I can't see it. But he'll tell me and that's helpful because it means my man will react in a certain way.

"In pass blocking, it is my job to pick up anybody who is loose. I'm the keeper for the rest of the guys. I do a lot of the calls but everyone makes them."

Ayers made the move from defense to offense his very first year in 1976, and, surprisingly enough, didn't encounter any difficulty in doing so.

"In a way that was good because I didn't have any bad habits as an offensive lineman when I came into the NFL," Ayers said. "I didn't know anything about blocking so I was able to learn the right way from scratch.

"But until 1979, I kept thinking of myself as

Tackle Dan Audick.

a displaced defensive lineman and that maybe any day they were going to put me back over there. Sometime during 1979 I started to feel comfortable as an offensive lineman. McKittrick teaches techniques in such a way that you feel like you are improving all the time. That is gratifying. It makes you want to work that much harder."

No one worked harder than Audick. He had been drafted and cut by Pittsburgh, signed and cut by Cleveland, signed and kept briefly by St. Louis, before winding up with San Diego. Between those jobs, he once wrestled a bear for $200 in Alexandria, Virginia. The 49ers obtained Audick before the 1981 season when Dan Bungarda went down with an injury and there wasn't anybody to replace him.

"We brought him in to start unless he just plain disappoints us," Walsh said at the time.

Considered small for a tackle, Audick nevertheless started every game for the 49ers. His size didn't bother McKittrick in the least.

"Dan is the least physical lineman for his position," McKittrick said. "He might be a little undersized for offensive guard. He is quick, though, and might have the best nasty streak on the unit, which I kind of like. He doesn't let you down."

The 49ers didn't have many down linemen in reserve, only center-guard Walt Downing, guard-tackle John Choma and tackle Allen Kennedy.

Apparently, they were all that was needed.

THE JACK REYNOLDS-FRED DEAN CONNECTION

They arrived as strangers in 1981, unwanted by the teams they'd played for previously. Both were driven by fierce pride, and were determined to prove their value. It was harder for Jack Reynolds. The veteran linebacker was 33, old by professional standards. The other, defensive end Fred Dean, was only 29. From the very first day he reported to training camp, Reynolds had to show the 49ers he could still perform at a high level. Dean didn't even join the team until the sixth week of the season, following a brief retirement—the result of a contract squabble with the San Diego Chargers. As it turned out, Reynolds and Dean were the links that had been missing from the 49er defense. With that chain complete, the 49ers went on to win 11 of their last 12 games of the 1981 season.

Reynolds was tense for the first few days of the 49ers' training session in Rocklin, 110 miles south of San Francisco. For 11 years he'd been considered the enemy there. Furthermore, he was the oldest player in camp and he knew there were some who felt he could not stand another hot, strenuous training grind followed by a long season. Still, he had a reputation as a hard-nosed linebacker and he was bent on keeping it.

Since 1970 Reynolds had been a vital part of the Los Angeles Rams' stony defense. Those were the Rams' glory years, when the team as much as owned the Western Division Championship. And during that time the rivalry between the Rams and the 49ers had been intense, extending beyond the playing field into the very council chambers of the two cities. There may never have been a fiercer rivalry in the National Football League. Now Reynolds was on the other side.

Three months earlier, in a disagreement over his contract, Reynolds had been unceremoniously dumped by the Rams. In this case, money wasn't as much an issue as the fact that the Rams would only offer him a one-year deal while Reynolds wanted three. There were many in the NFL who felt the Rams were making an example of Reynolds during their contract negotiations and that their refusal to give him a new long-term contract was intended to serve as a warning to other veterans who were thinking along the same lines. Was Reynolds, who had been Los Angeles' starting middle linebacker for eight campaigns and an All-Pro for three of those seasons, asking too much? Some thought so, for suddenly, and at an advanced point in his career, Reynolds found

himself a free agent.

It looked for a while as though he would sign with the Buffalo Bills. The reasons were obvious. For one thing, the Bills were considered a legitimate playoff contender for the 1981 season. Another reason was more personal: Reynolds had played most of his career with the Rams under Chuck Know who was now the head coach at Buffalo. Then there was linebacker Isiah Robertson, who had played alongside Reynolds at Los Angeles. Robertson had also had a contract dispute with the Rams, and moved over to the Bills in 1979.

But Bill Walsh had other plans for Reynolds. In his third year as coach of the 49ers, Walsh was ready to make a major change in his defense. The Niners had played some 3-4 and some 4-3 the year before, but as strategical trends in professional football changed, Walsh came to prefer the 3-4. With someone of Reynolds' stature, he'd be able to employ it effectively for the 1981 campaign.

Reynolds was not only experienced and savvy, but Walsh felt he could provide leadership for the 49ers' young defense. Over the objections of his defensive coordinator Chuck Studley, who was among those who felt Reynolds was too old, Walsh signed Reynolds a month before training camp opened.

Then, the very first day at Rocklin, Studley's doubts were reinforced when Reynolds hurt his knee. Though it wasn't serious, it was enough to slow him down at a time when he was anxious to impress the coaching staff of his new team. It wasn't until several days later, after his knee had responded to treatment, that he felt like himself again, and broke through the tension.

The 49ers were working on pass rushing drills. The coaches positioned a tackling dummy, in place of a quarterback, in the backfield where a passer would normally set up. When it was Reynolds' turn to rush, he had to get by a big young lineman as fast as possible in order to "overtake" the dummy. At the signal Reynolds charged. He met the blocker head on, knocked him off his feet and jumped over him. He wasn't finished. Reynolds continued straight to his objective and bowled it over, all within the time limit.

Walsh was impressed. But Reynolds' performance didn't go unnoticed by Studley either, who was looking on with a more critical eye.

"For the life of me, I couldn't see what Bill wanted with a 33-year-old guy who, as far as I could see, would do nothing but take the place of a younger player," he said later. "I was wrong. Once I saw him in training camp, I knew he was the man we needed."

What the 49ers had needed as part of their new defensive strategy was an inside linebacker who could play the run effectively. From a standpoint of technique, this was new to Reynolds, who had been a middle linebacker all his career and an exceptional one at that. He had all but led the Rams in tackles every year. Since he'd made his career as a bounty hunter—searching out running backs—Reynolds was hoping to be utilized as the strong-side inside linebacker opposite the tight end, behind whom most runners go. Yet it was Walsh's intention to position Reynolds as

A determined Reynolds zeroes in on Houston's Earl Campbe

the weakside inside linebacker.

"I'll just have to wade through more garbage to get to the ball," said Reynolds when he first learned of Walsh's plans. "Bill Bergey is a tackler like me and I think Philadelphia plays him on the strong side in their 3-4."

Walsh was looking beyond that. He didn't look at Reynolds as a one-year player. He expected him to perform for several more years, and he sold that concept to his new linebacker without making any long overtures.

"This gives him an opportunity to extend his career," he explained. "In a 4-3 defense like the Rams use, middle linebackers take an awful beating and it gets worse toward the end of their career, especially in the longer 16-game schedule. As we go along, Jack will find that he has more access to the runner from this inside weak position. He'll be unblocked more often as he comes across from the backside. He'll get into the pursuit faster, and that's one of the best things he does."

During his first few weeks with the new team, Reynolds didn't want to discuss his feelings about the treatment he'd received from the Rams. He didn't want to get into any mud slinging. What he wanted was to help the 49ers win. He was wary about interviews and was polite but firm in refusing to do one with a television crew from Los Angeles.

"What good would it do me to stab them in the back now?" he asked. "The only thing I tried to do was help those people and it wasn't good enough. I felt I could play longer and help more here than anywhere else. I liked Bill's imagination on offense. It was hard to defense against San Francisco when I played with the Rams. I liked the way Paul Hofer ran the ball and I knew Joe Montana was going to develop.

"They probably figured I was a goldbrick the first few days, that I was too old to play. But I don't think Bill thought that. In football it doesn't matter how old you are. The question is, can you get the job done? The last year or so that Isiah Robertson was with us on the Rams, he quit running full speed so he lost his 'quickness. It doesn't matter how big or tall you are. Anything physical begins with the mind. The mind rules the body."

Now Reynolds wanted to close the book on

Reynolds checks an autograph for an admiring fan.

Los Angeles. The only thing he brought with him when he went to the 49ers was his film projector. When George Allen coached the Rams for a brief period before the 1978 season, he had shown Reynolds how much you can learn by watching game films. Reynolds went out and bought his own projector and now he's a film addict. Nobody spends more time in the dark, reliving each play, than Reynolds—including the coaching staff.

He's the first one to report for practice each day. Sometimes he's so early that he makes a pot of coffee and he'll often end up drinking most of it because he's usually the last to leave. He practically lives at the practice facility. He works out, watches film, studies some more, takes a sauna and finally goes home. He often follows the same routine on Tuesday while the rest of his teammates are enjoying a day off.

"The reason I watch films and study so hard is simple," he explains. "You *can* be taught to a certain extent. There are guys blessed with more football instinct or talent. But, if you incorporate that with studying and watching films, you can go from there. I watch films to

see what I've done wrong and what the team has done wrong, then correct it. I spend a lot of time at it. The more you know about the opponent the better you play. Sometimes you watch so many films your head spins. I watch no more than three reels at the same time, but I'll watch one play over and over again, front-wards and backwards."

Reynolds has always been deadly serious about football. In 1969, while in college at the University of Tennessee, he acquired his nickname "Hacksaw" in a feat that has since become part of Tennessee football lore. He cut a 1953 Chevrolet in half using a small hand saw following a frustrating loss to the University of Mississippi and has retained the nickname ever since.

On game days Reynolds can't get to the stadium early enough. He'd be there at 7 a.m. if they opened the gates. On Sunday morning before a game, when Studley always conducts

a defensive team meeting, Reynolds attends in his uniform, more or less ready to play. In order to do so he takes his uniform with him after Saturday practice, dresses at home, and reaches the stadium suited up.

"To save time, speed the process and keep up with my own schedule, I'm dressed and taped when I get to the meeting," he says.

"When people see me in a car, driving to the stadium dressed in a 49er jersey, they figure it's some nut of a fan."

When the 49ers were in Los Angeles during the regular 1981 season to face the Rams for a second time, after beating them 20-17 a month earlier, Reynolds attended church early on the morning of the game—a fact that may not seem unusual except that he went to church with his ankles and hands taped. The 49ers then defeated the Rams for the second time, 33-31. It was the first time they had accomplished a sweep since 1965.

That win was especially significant for Reynolds for two reasons. First, because he was celebrating his 34th birthday and what better way to do so; and second, he played one of his finest games of the season. He left the Ram fans moaning after racking up 16 tackles against his former teammates. Reynolds hadn't been forgotten. Banners with his nickname on them were hung around the stadium, and a small airplane flew overhead with birthday greetings.

By that season's end he'd given the 49ers the leadership they needed by showing them how to win and had led the club in tackles with 117. He set the pattern in two early season games when he made 12 tackles against the Chicago Bears on September 13, and 13 against the New Orleans Saints on September 27.

"I thought in years past that in some ways the 49ers were afraid to succeed," said Reynolds. "I guess 1979 was Bill's first year as coach, but we [the Rams] only beat the 49ers by three points both times we played them and had to come from behind to do it. They always had the offense. Now the defense has been rebuilt and I think both teams complement each other. No matter how much talent you have, though, the players have got to want to do it. That's the number-one thing. The coaching has to be good, but if your players want to play, no matter what the situation is, they're going to play."

Reynolds showed them what dedication can accomplish. Certainly, no one worked harder. His consuming desire to play rubbed off on the others, and Studley was the first to recognize it.

"Jack Reynolds is the hardest-working guy on our team, by far," he says. "He takes voluminous notes on everything. He watches more game film than some of our coaches. He takes our game plan and our scouting report each week (and that would be 50 or 60 pages), and then he copies them in longhand. Then he goes over it and over it.

"There are a lot of linebackers in the NFL who are bigger or stronger or faster or all three. Jack offsets that with his intensity. It's corny, but he's literally a coach on the field, and a lot of things we do on the field we couldn't do without Jack."

To Fred Dean, who started the season with the San Diego Chargers, it looked as though the 1981 season would turn out to be a nightmare. He was disillusioned with football, and his contract with the Chargers was at the root of his discontent.

After the 1979 season the NFL Management Council had issued a report on player salaries and Dean had learned that, at $67,525 a year, he was playing for less money than anyone else in his position. That was despite having been a two-time All-Pro and the American Football Conference's Defensive Player of the Year in 1979. He wanted a new contract—one that would bring his salary up to the level prescribed by the league's own standards.

To demonstrate his unhappiness with his 1980 contract, which paid him $75,000, as part of a multi-year contract, Dean sat out the

Chargers' first three games of the season. Then management convinced him to come back by promising to work on his contract with his attorney, David Perrine, during the season, and to have their differences resolved when it ended. But when Dean reported to the Chargers for the 1981 campaign, his contract hadn't been changed. This gnawed at him, but he still kept his feelings private. Then, in San Diego's opening game against the Cleveland Browns, Dean pulled a groin muscle and injured his sternum, causing him to miss the following week's game against Detroit. He returned for the third week against Kansas City but failed to show up for practice during the week. Then he managed to report in time for the game against Denver and played the entire contest.

Dean was growing increasingly unhappy. He heard that some club officials were saying he wasn't extending himself on the field, which hurt his pride. Finally, on October 1, 1981 he couldn't take it any more and decided to call a press conference to announce his retirement. By coincidence, on the very same day, the Chargers also called a press conference, an hour earlier than Dean's, and announced the acquisition of wide receiver Wes Chandler from New Orleans. That overshadowed Dean's announcement, but he got his message across.

"I have continued to play in the hopes that these differences could be resolved," he said. "Apparently, they are not going to be. I'm not asking that I be the highest paid defensive lineman but I am asking that my salary be brought to the standard of my playing ability."

Dean had decided to return to his home in Ruston, Louisiana and continue his education at Louisiana Tech, but said he would continue his workouts with the hope that the Chargers might work out a trade for him. Otherwise, at the age of 29, he faced the prospect of not playing for two years until his present contract expired. Unfortunately, four weeks of the season were gone and Dean wasn't optimistic.

"I was down and out," he said, recalling the two weeks he spent at home. "Those days were kind of rough. I read a lot, I drank a lot. I'd given up hope of playing football this season. It got to where it didn't even matter."

However, it did matter to the 49ers. By this time, after starting the season at 1-2, they had improved their record to 3-2. Walsh was convinced his offense was producing to playoff potential, but felt the defense needed more help. He was most concerned about the pass rush. So when he learned that Dean, one of the most feared pass rushers in the NFL, was looking for a new team, he worked out a deal with San Diego immediately, giving the Chargers a second round draft choice in 1983 for the rights to Dean's contract.

Walsh's move surprised everyone because Dean had always operated from a 4-3 alignment. The 49ers were committed to using a 3-4. Would Dean be effective in a 3-4? The skeptics had had the same question when Walsh signed Reynolds earlier in the season. In that case, after five weeks of play, with Reynolds leading the team in tackles, the critics had been silenced.

In the end, Walsh's decision to acquire Dean is testimony to his vision. He felt that by acquiring Dean, he would be able to go all out in the chase for a spot in the playoffs. Nobody else would have given the 49ers a chance at it. Walsh was convinced that, like Reynolds, Dean could help fill out the defense without changing his alignment at all.

"We now have a very competitive defense," he said after Dean had moved over. "We have a lot of alternatives. It's not as though we'll have to come up with some new style of defense."

Walsh envisioned using Dean as a skilled pass rusher in obvious passing situations. He didn't intend to start Dean at all, but to keep him fresh on the sidelines so he would be as effective in the fourth period as in the beginning of the game. He would insert Dean into the lineup either on a second and long situation or in a definite third down passing predicament. The pressure Dean could exert on opposing quarterbacks was a weapon the 49ers had been lacking for the first five games.

Offensive tackle Keith Fahnhorst was delighted that Dean had signed with the 49ers. "There aren't many defensive ends around like Fred Dean," he said. "I remember playing against him in an exhibition game in 1975 when he was a rookie with the Chargers. I

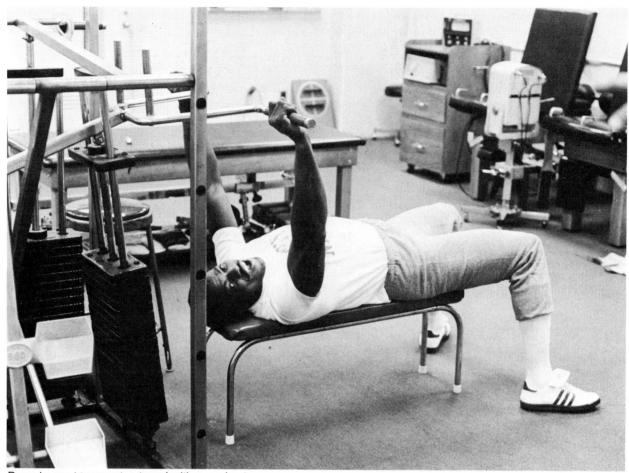
Dean keeps his muscles toned with a workout.

looked in the program and saw 6-2, 230 pounds. I licked my chops. On the very first play he flew by me so fast I never saw him. I asked someone, 'Who the hell is that guy?' "

The Dallas Cowboys were asking the same thing after their sixth game of the season, when San Francisco had routed them, 45-14. Defensive line coach Bill McPherson had worked hard with Dean in preparation for that game but since Dean had kept himself in good shape, he was able to concentrate on parlance and getting his timing honed.

Dean played even more than he'd expected in the game against the Cowboys. When San Francisco jumped into an early lead, it meant that Dallas had to rely more on its passing attack. So the 49ers used a 4-3 and a 4-2-5 in obvious passing situations. They liked what they saw in Dean that day. He pressured Dallas quarterback Danny White seven times and was credited with three tackles, two passes defensed, and two sacks. White had felt Dean's presence throughout the game. In one series Dean had pressured him three times in a row. He also made it clear that he could play the run.

"It is remarkable," said McPherson afterward. "They ran a trap at him and he made the tackle. Then they ran a draw and he made the tackle. Then they tried a pitch to his side, and again he made the tackle.

Dean took it all in stride. He had been such a force in that first game that the 49ers wanted to figure out a way to use him more. They started to think about overshifting the defensive line, placing three linemen to one side with Dean by himself on the other, and an inside linebacker plugging the hole in between. Walsh was intrigued by the possibilities and they tried it the following week against Green Bay. Dean responded with two tackles and a sack. A week later, against the Los Angeles Rams, Dean really erupted. He recorded a career high of 4½ sacks in that 20-17

Coach Bill Walsh makes a point to the muscular Dean.

victory, practically destroying the Rams' All-Pro tackle, Doug France. Dean still wasn't totally satisfied with his performance.

"On a scale of one to ten," I rate my performance an eight," he said.

His teammates had a higher opinion of him, seeing how he was influencing their defense. In a five week period, San Francisco defeated Dallas, Green Bay, Los Angeles, Pittsburgh and Atlanta. The rest of the league started to take note of the team.

Reynolds, whose situation was similar to Dean's, said, "As far as I'm concerned, Fred Dean should be in the game on every play. I'm not happy sitting on the bench any more than I am now. But I guess if we win, that's the important thing."

"It's the type of problem you really don't mind having," Walsh added. "I know Jack would like to be in there on every play. He's that type of player, but you have to make some adjustments sometimes. As far as Fred is con-

cerned, we're working him into the system slowly. We don't want to change things too quickly or mess up what we've built. You never know what kind of situation is going to present itself, so we just have to wait and see."

Dwaine Board, who moves over from right end to tackle when Dean comes into the game, saw a lot of his new teammate in the Pittsburgh game, which the 49ers won, 17-14.

"I still can't believe Fred in that game," he said. "They were double-teaming him and when they got confused nobody blocked me. So I had a clear shot and still couldn't beat Fred to the quarterback. As I went for the sack, he was right there, too."

Dan Audick, the 49ers left tackle, knows how Dean operates, having faced him many times in 49er practices. "This man possesses so much speed and strength, it's incredible," he says. "He's the only player I've played against where I've literally seen stars after blocking him."

"The last piece of the puzzle was Fred Dean," adds defensive end Jim Stuckey. "He made everything click and elevated the play of the other linemen. He came in here and everyone was set in their routines. We were all thinking, 'Who's place is Fred going to take? Who's going to get cut?' After his first practice I was thinking, 'God, how can this guy be so little yet so dominating?' It must be his long arms."

Free safety Dwight Hicks, who sees Dean from the secondary, adds that, "Dean is so good that he inspires the rest of us. He is no ordinary man. Fred Dean is the best defensive end in football. He is that good. You watch Joe Klecko (New York Jets) and Fred Dean and make your own distinctions. Run two projectors at the same time and you'll see. I'm not taking anything away from Klecko, but Dean is the best."

It didn't take 49er fans long to catch on to Dean, and their chants of "Dean-fence" began to reverberate throughout Candlestick Park. The phrase refers to the time in high school when Dean grabbed an opposing quarterback and threw him under a fence at one side of the field. It wasn't long after that that Dean picked up the nickname "Mean."

"I love my nickname when it's applied to football," says Dean, "but I'm not a bad person. I take out my aggressions on the football field, where it's legal. This doesn't mean I want to hurt people in football. I just love the challenge of beating the guy across from me. That's what football is all about."

Dean has a lot of pluck. It's one of his most admirable characteristics, and one that was most obvious when Dean had a shooting accident in 1974, his senior year in college. "I was cleaning out a gun and there was a bullet still in the chamber," he recalls. "The gun fired and the bullet went to the left of my abdomen. I spent about 30 minutes in the hospital, just long enough for them to dig out the bullet and clean out the wound. I had to go to practice."

Dean was considered small even for a college end. He only weighed 205 pounds and that was after he'd been on a weight program that added 30 pounds to his frame. Still, he had to convince the coaches that he was big enough to play defensive end.

"I've had to prove myself all along, starting in high school, because of my size," he explains. "I weighed only 175 pounds in high school, but I played all over the place. I played offensive tackle, offensive guard, defensive end, all over. But I was blessed with good speed and good strength and I guess that made up for my size." In his four years at Tech he made All-Southland Conference each year, and his team won 44 of 48 games.

San Diego thought enough of Dean to make him a second round draft choice in 1975. However, because of his size, they valued him as a linebacker. He soon changed their minds.

"It was all new to me and besides, I still thought I could play defensive end as a pro," says Dean. "I figured I would be playing second or third string as a linebacker. One day I decided to have a talk with coach Tommy Prothro. I told him how I felt about it and he finally told me to give it a try. I guess he liked what he saw because I've been a defensive end ever since.

"In San Diego, the 4-3 was all I played. Here the techniques are totally different, but I can adjust to them. I believe in what I'm doing and I feel I can do it better than anyone else. There's not a big guy I can't be adequate against, even against the run. The way I feel about it, there's a place in the world for us little people. In the future I'd like to play more. My role is to sack the quarterback and stop the run. I don't care what defense the 49ers use or how they use me. I know my role. I know why they brought me here. I love it. It's really easy on passing situations. You just put your head down and go after the quarterback.

"It's like a tremendous burden was lifted from my shoulders coming here. I felt I had something to prove to San Diego. I invested a lot of time there. I was always double-teamed. I just wasn't appreciated.

"The Chargers made me realize that no matter how much fun football is, it's a business, not a game. The 49ers gave me a chance to play. When I came here I felt I could contribute to this team. When I left San Diego, I left a really good team, but it wasn't hard to leave because I wasn't happy there. I'm happy here."

THE DEFENSE

It was obvious things were going to be different when the 49ers reported to the 1981 summer camp on an oppressive day in July. There were so many new faces. Everybody knew linebacker Jack Reynolds, even though this was his first camp with the Niners. After all, he had played with Los Angeles for the past eleven years. But there was no other way to look upon the four rookies except as total strangers. In a bold, unprecedented move, Walsh had drafted four defensive backs on his first five selections in the 1981 college draft.

Personnel directors around the league were laughing at Walsh. Nobody had ever done what he had done. But it was not an impetuous maneuver. The plan was conceived after untold hours of strategy sessions with his defensive aides, namely Chuck Studley, the overall defensive coordinator, and George Seifert, whose sole area of responsibility was the defensive backfield. They reasoned that the 49ers had given up 416 points in 1979, and 415 points in 1980, which was no improvement at all. The secondary was at best a revolving door of transients. In 1979 alone, 32 defensive backs had passed through San Francisco. Their shortcomings were evident. In

1979, the Niners finished 24th in the NFL; the following year, they finished 27th. In fact, in 1980 they set the unenviable record for allowing opposition teams to complete 66.1 per cent of their passes, the highest in league history. That's when Walsh and his staff decided to go all out and draft defensive backs. The move also reflected an evolution of defensive philosophy.

New rules for offensive blocking on passing plays allowed receivers more time to get open. The fact that they could be bumped only once—within five yards of the line of scrimmage—made speedy wide receivers a most dangerous weapon. It would take an enormous effort by the defensive linemen to minimize the chance of a completion on every passing play. Thus San Francisco's defensive strategists believed the emphasis on pass defense had to be where the passes would be thrown, in the secondary.

"I used to think it all started up front," Studley revealed, "but with the rules changes that permitted offensive linemen almost unrestricted use of their hands and arms in pass blocking that's all changed. Now, I think the game begins on the corners. You must have people who can cover the corners. You used to

Line coach Bill McPherson makes a point with defensive end Bill Stuckey.

be able to get by with a damn good pass rush. You've got world class sprinters for wide receivers so you've got to have defensive people who can stay with them.

"You're going to see more and more defensive backs on the field. Sometimes you see three and four wide receivers in the game. So you'll see six and seven defensive backs. How can you hope to cover a fast wide receiver with a slow linebacker? It can't be done. As it turned out, Bill made a wise decision. You can't get an adequate rush with a four-man line. You really can't rush anymore. Take Dallas with their dominating line. Look at

their pass defense statistics. They're not that good. You must have people who are prepared to play man-to-man coverage. Zones are inadequate. You just have to have people who can cover."

So the 49ers acted. At the college draft that spring, they made Ronnie Lott, a 6'0" safety from USC their number-one selection; Eric Wright, a 6'1" safety from Missouri was their second pick on round two; Carlton Williamson, a 6'0" safety from Pittsburgh, came on round three; and Lynn Thomas, a 5'11" cornerback also from Pittsburgh, was acquired on round five. The selections made waves

Linebacker Keena Turner.

throughout the NFL.

"I really didn't know what to think," Seifert said. "This was something Bill felt we had to do, and I think justifiably so. And once that decision was made, there was no opportunity to think about what was going to happen."

Walsh wasn't overly concerned. "It's a calculated risk," he said. "And there weren't any real alternatives."

Walsh was hoping that three of the four rookies would blend in with the sole remaining member of the secondary, Dwight Hicks. The 6'1" safety had been a flop with two other teams before Walsh picked him up as a free

agent in 1979. Yet, with less than two full seasons of experience, Hicks was classified as a veteran. The two years he spent in San Francisco's weak secondary in 1979 and 1980 were the equivalent of four years elsewhere.

It remained to be seen how the rookies would mesh into the system. It was unorthodox chemistry. The beginning was wild. Everyone was bumping into everyone else in practice during the early weeks of training camp. Slowly they began to come together as a unit. And by the time the 49ers played their first pre-season game against the Seattle Seahawks, Walsh was confident that he had a respectable secondary.

"They played like they were real performers," Walsh said. "They weren't distracted, and they didn't show a lack of confidence or concentration. They went out and played like they had played in college. They didn't even think about whether it was professional ball or not."

Hicks was a major reclamation project. After his abbreviated careers with the Detroit Lions and the Philadelphia Eagles, Hicks wound up managing a health food store in Southfield, Michigan. In October, 1979, the Niners put in a call to him and persuaded him to return to pro football. He became the mainstay of the 49ers' beleaguered secondary until the draft infusion of 1981.

"When I was cut from the Eagles in 1979, after I thought I had made the team, I was shocked, stunned," Hicks said. "One of the assistant coaches told me he thought it was a bad mistake, that I could play in the NFL. But I told him, 'It's easy for you to say that. You're not the one who has to make a living.' I was really wondering about my future. I felt I had wasted a lot of time. I asked myself if it was worth keeping after. But my wife, Josefa, told me to look at it like baseball. In baseball you get three strikes before you're out. I had only two strikes."

The third time around he made it. The 49ers had a different opinion of Hicks. And they turned out to be right.

"You have to give credit to our staff, especially John McVay and Tony Razzano, for being so thorough and having good judgment," Walsh said. "Sometimes, too, other

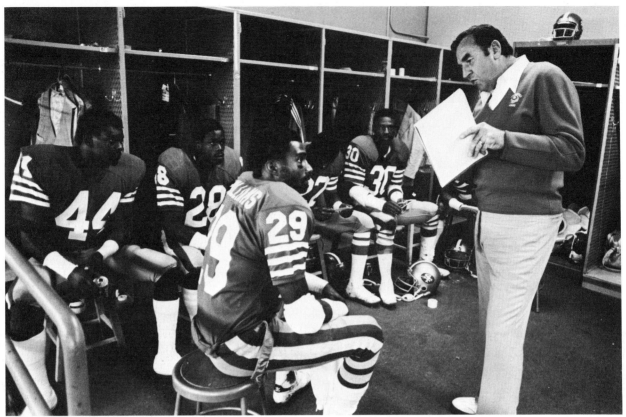
Linebacker coach Norb Hecker diagrams an alignment.

people have made mistakes. It's hard to believe that teams that had Dwight Hicks couldn't see his ability. We looked at hundreds of free agents. The ones who are around now are the cream of the crop. There are NFL players who take two or three training camps to really learn their trade.

"The first year, they don't make it at all. The second year, they come close, but still aren't quite ready to play. And the experience they have gotten from a couple of pro training camps is much more valuable than what they learned in their college careers. That's why it's so misleading when, for instance, you see a story that says some team made a mistake on a player because they released him and he made a team somewhere else. A team may very well think a player has a chance to make it in another year or two, but they can't afford to keep him and wait for him to make it.

"Hicks improved immeasurably in 1980 and played extremely fine football," Walsh continued. "He was the team's top tackling defensive back. He is the soundest tackler on the team, is very intelligent and understands cov-erages and receiver routes."

Hicks led the 49ers in interceptions with nine in 1981. He also set a team record for most interception return yardage in a season with 239. His 104 yards in interception returns in one game also established a club record. He set one more record, too. In a game against Washington, Hicks recovered a fumble and ran 80 yards for a touchdown. And after recording ten solo tackles against the Los Angeles Rams, the 49er secondary became known as "Dwight Hicks and his Hot Licks." It wasn't that easy in the beginning, though.

"I was very skeptical at first," Hicks said. "Yet, I never felt I had to lead these guys around, show them anything, just because they're all rookies. They're all excellent athletes. It was definitely a factor to their immediate adjustment that they came out of big schools, big programs. Playing in the Bowl games, being in the media nationally, it sort of prepares you for the pros.

"Seifert is like a college professor in his teaching method. We do a lot of blackboard work. He believes that if you know your de-

Dwaine Board consoles Archie Reese.

fenses very well, the less you have to think out there, the more you can react. The blackboard and practice might be tiring, it might be boring. But, the more you go over it, the better you know it.

"With the talent we had, and the way George and Ray Rhodes worked with us, we gained confidence so fast that by the fifth game we didn't even consider ourselves rookies any more. We worked hard and long. We had more meetings than any other unit. We went over things until we literally knew them in our sleep. Really, I was nodding off during one meeting, in a daze, and George asked me a question. I swear I answered correctly without even waking up."

What shook up the entire NFL was the 49ers' draft of Lott on the first round. He was the eighth player selected overall and was considered a blue-chip prospect by the pro scouts. Even before Lott reported to the Niners, Walsh had a high opinion of him.

"He may just be the best athlete on the club," Walsh said.

Dick Steinberg, the player personnel director of the New England Patriots, went even further in his appraisal of Lott's ability.

"He's a guy who comes along once every five or six years," Steinberg said. "He's a catalyst-type guy who makes other people play better."

It was one reason why the young secondary blended together so effectively. Lott turned out to be just that, a catalyst. Not only did he intercept seven passes, turning three of them into touchdowns, but he was beaten only once for a touchdown all season long. Nobody could have played the corner better. The rest of the secondary picked up the tempo. They certainly didn't look like rookies.

"We come from schools where it's really hard to accept defeat," Lott said. "USC, Pitt, Michigan—you win there. You learn early about that winning tradition, and you start believing in it. It becomes a part of you. And I think that made us push each other. We helped each other. We are a bunch of young guys, to tell you the truth, who don't know our place. They say we were rookies, but I question it. It seems like we've already played together. Sometimes, I really wonder if it would have worked with, let's say, three veterans and one

rookie or any other combination. I think we've been able to help each other more this way.

"Oh, it was a joke during pre-season. Just awful. We didn't know what we were doing. We'd bump into each other on coverages and we'd blow assignments all the time. That made it very easy to get discouraged. But we knew that regardless of what we did, the coaches were going to stick with us. Man, I didn't want to get beat all year.

"I think when the rules were changed to help the offense, people were afraid guys were just going to blow right by us. People got scared when the bump-and-run was taken away. But most patterns today are timing patterns. So if you can bump a receiver out of his pattern for even a second, you're starting even with him."

On the field, Lott is tenacious. He is not afraid to hit, which, in turn, plants fear in ambitious receivers. Yet, off the field, Lott is a different person. It's hard to imagine, but he is low-key and softspoken, almost to the point of being shy.

"I've never been the type of person who could just walk into a place and light up the room," Lott said. "People don't know who you are in this business, especially when they see you away from the football field. They expect you to act like some sort of jock. They don't think that you can communicate with the rest of the world. I'm human, just like everybody else. When I leave the field, I leave my image there, too.

"I'm always driving down the road and switching the radio dial for a good jazz station to carry me along. If I'm listening to a good set of songs in my car, then I might keep driving for days. It's as if I'm in a trance. And that's the way I relax at home, too. I sit around listening to music. Music is a way I can gear myself down. I can sit back and reflect on the day. I think of myself as a mellow person.

"Jazz is unique. Unlike rock and roll, or rhythm and blues, or any other type of music, you can experience what's going on with jazz. It's perfect for me. I've never played an instrument before in my life. I've always wanted to play the piano, though; and I eventually will take piano lessons some day."

Apparently Lott didn't need many lessons

Linebacker Craig Puki.

Linebacker Dan Bunz.

Linebacker Bobby Leopold.

Linebacker Milt McColl.

on the field to make the transition from college safety to pro cornerback. From the first day he walked on the gridiron of Sierra College for his first professional training camp, players and coaches alike recognized his talents.

"I knew Ronnie could play when I saw his first practice," Walsh said. "A great athlete. And while he weighs more than 205, he plays like a 180 pounder. A great hitter, great shocker, an instinctive performer. He is one of the best players in the league."

Hicks liked Lott, too.

"I knew he could play the first time I ever saw him," Hicks said.

Then there was Eric Wright, who played safety in college at Missouri. The 49er braintrust didn't worry about switching him to cornerback. They thought so highly of him they made him their second selection in the two second round picks they had. He, too, had a reputation as a hitter and had an outstanding career in college.

"We feel Wright can play cornerback in the NFL," Walsh commented after the draft. "He was a free safety throughout college but has the speed and ability to be a pro corner."

Known as the "other cornerback," Wright had three interceptions and was sixth on the team in number of tackles with 75. It was soon clear that the 49er secondary was aggressive almost to the point of intimidation.

"Intimidation?" Wright asked. "Well, that's the label people put on us, but I'm not sure it's accurate. We just go out to do our jobs, and if we have to get physical doing them, well . . ."

Before the first Los Angeles game in October, which the 49ers won, 20-17, the secondary was going through some forceful drills. Perhaps too much so. The coaches felt it was time to interrupt the workouts before somebody got hurt.

"They told us to take it a little easier in practice," Wright said. "They said we had a tendency to be aggressive. But we came a long way. I remember during training camp when the veterans tried to get us to do a rookie show. We just wouldn't do it. If they were going to make one of us do it, they were going to have to make all of us do it. I don't like anybody coming and telling me what to do.

We just like our personalities and it shows."

The only one of the three brash rookies who remained at his usual position was Carlton Williamson. Drafted on the third round, Williamson had played safety at Pitt. Originally he came to Pittsburgh as a fullback after playing quarterback in high school. However, he switched to the defensive backfield as a sophomore just to make the travelling squad. By his junior year, he was a starter and led the Panthers in tackles the last two years he played.

"At Pitt we had something called the Ding Dong Award," Williamson said. "It was for the best hit of the week. Hugh Green and Ricky Jackson collected most of them, but I got my share.

"We've gotten all kinds of nicknames. 'Dwight Hicks and his Hot Licks' is one that is real popular. Some guys on the team call me 'The Hammer.' It's a matter of, if you see a shot, take it. We don't make late hits. We just zero in on targets."

But how could playoff-type maturity be acquired by a group of rookies, regardless of the talent each possessed? That was the dilemma facing Studley and his defensive aide Seifert. There is no short cut to experience and, by all counts, an inexperienced secondary is often an Achilles heel. Had the 49ers taken too big a gamble? Weeks of blackboard cramming and practice during training camp would be the determining factor. That's how the coaching staff approached the defensive unit that could make or break the 1981 season.

"Talent and hard work," Seifert said. "It wasn't as though we were rebuilding the secondary. It was more like building from scratch, using Hicks as the foundation and surrounding him with young, eager, talented people. They knew from the start they were going to go through hot water together and would have to grow and learn together. In that way it was a blessing, because we all started on the same page. The idea was to keep everything as simple as possible and progress chapter by chapter. But after five games they were doing so well, playing with such confidence, that we were able to throw the book at them.

"Hicks is our quarterback on defense. He

Defensive backfield coach George Seifert shows how he wants it done.

calls the coverages for linebackers and defensive backs. He is technique-conscious and aware of everything around him. Lott is strong and has quick, basketball type moves. He has a great innate feel. If he were a quarterback, he would always find the open receiver. If he were a running back, he would get to that little crack in the line that others might not even see. Wright is cat-quick with excellent range and a good jumper. He has a willingness to commit his body, just like all of our guys. What turned us on when we saw Williamson at Pitt was his intensity. He came to us as a tremendous hitter with deceptive speed and has developed into a good pass defender."

The final step in the shaping of the defen-

sive backs was entrusted to Ray Rhodes, Seifert's assistant who had played the 1980 season with San Francisco after spending six years with the New York Giants—the first three as a wide receiver. He translated Seifert's teachings into play-action by demonstrating technique as a former defender himself. Since he was still young enough to play, the players related to him. This was important during games, when Rhodes was part of the sideline action and Seifert dictated strategy high above the playing field from the scouting booth.

"After every series I talk to Ray on the headphones about adjustments," Seifert said. "Then he tells each player. That's a great set-up, because usually you tell one of the players, who is preoccupied with his own duties. So you would lose a lot when he tried to tell the other players what to do. Consistency, technique, understanding. We can still improve in those areas. They will get better."

It is hard to imagine. In one word, they were simply "awesome" rookies. The 49ers' calculated risk, as Walsh described it, yielded high returns.

"I think the suddenness with which they developed into good people surprised all of us," Studley said. "You think they're good now? Wait until they really learn the game."

The 49er defensive unit had a decidedly youthful look in other positions, too. Only three players, linebackers Willie Harper and Dan Bunz and tackle Archie Reese were around before 1979, the year Walsh took over. Hicks and end Dwaine Board joined the club in 1979. The rest of the secondary included cornerback Lynn Thomas, who was drafted on the fifth round of the 1981 draft, cornerback Saladin Martin and safety Rick Gervais, who were both signed as free agents in 1981.

Walsh was not averse to signing free agents, providing they exerted a positive influence on his young team. The biggest acquisition was Jack Reynolds, a veteran linebacker who had been released by the Los Angeles Rams.

Reynolds was a key addition. The 49ers planned to utilize a three man front with four linebackers. They looked to Reynolds, one of the hardest tacklers in the league, to provide experience and leadership. Although he wasn't as fast at 33 as he once was, Reynolds would operate at an inside linebacker spot and do what he does best—stop the run.

The only other linebacker with any measurable experience was Willie Harper. In his eight years with San Francisco, only once did he play on a team that won more games than they lost. It could frustrate a guy. But the wave of new, young players gave Harper something positive to hope for, especially playing alongside Reynolds.

"I don't feel old," the 31-year-old Harper said. "I don't act old. I'm still in the prime of my career. I can still perform at the level expected. I feel like I'm one of the younger players."

Harper was a second round draft pick in

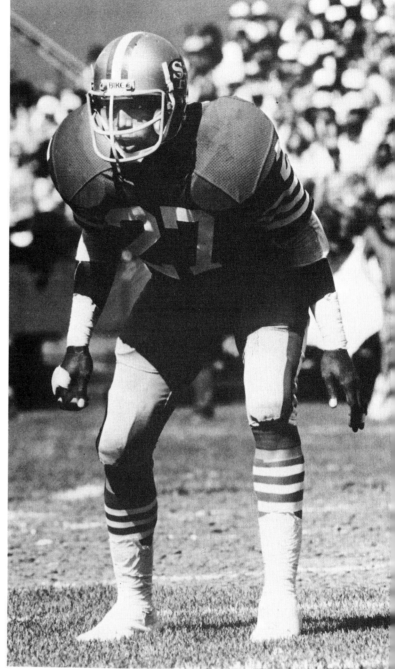

Safety Carlton Williamson.

1973. By the fourth game of his rookie season, he became a starter. At 6'2", 215 pounds, Harper is quick, which is necessary to play the outside. At Nebraska, he played running back and middle guard before moving over to defensive end.

"Harper had an excellent year in 1980, although he had an ankle injury late in the season," Walsh said. "He is a steady veteran with excellent ability, a mainstay on the 49er de-

Punter Jim Miller.

fense. He provides maturity and stability to the defense."

Unfortunately, Harper had been hampered by injuries most of his career. His most serious was in 1978, when he missed the entire season with an injured knee. Although his other injuries weren't as debilitating, they were troublesome. Still, Harper looked at it quite philosophically.

"Injuries are part of the game; that's why we wear pads," Harper said. "I have had my share, but no more than my share. The important thing is to keep coming back. That's what I did and I saw those young guys in the defensive backfield had the coverage down cold. They weren't missing anything. After that, we knew we could beat anybody."

Harper's back-up in 1980 was Keena Turner. He was drafted on the second round out of Purdue. When Harper was sidelined for four games, Turner filled in and made a good impression. Like Harper, he was quick and could run. At 6'2", 219 pounds, he was built along the same lines.

"Turner plays comparable football to Harper," Walsh said. "Some would even say, superior football."

The remaining member of the linebacker unit was Craig Puki, who played inside alongside Turner and next to Reynolds. It was like a dream come true for the second year linebacker. Drafted on the third round in 1980, Puki had also attended Tennessee and idolized Reynolds. The veteran Reynolds took Puki under his wing, roomed with him on the road, and kept teaching his young protege the finer points of linebacking—even if he did sound pessimistic about the team's chances.

"Jack kept saying during training camp that we would be lucky to win three games," Puki said, "and even when we started winning all those games he remained a pessimist. Actually, I'll start worrying about Jack when he says everything is all right. Then I'll know he's sick or something. Being pessimistic is his way of getting mentally prepared for everything.

"I've learned an awful lot from Jack. He's like a big brother to me. He teaches me everything from how to tie my shoes and take aspirin before a game to the deep strategy involved in football, like a tackle leaning the

Coach Bill Walsh

Joe Montana

Dwight Clark

Fred Solomon

Charle Young

Ricky Patton

Earl Cooper

Keith Fahnhorst

Randy Cross

Fred Dean

Jack Reynolds

Willie Harper

Keena Turner

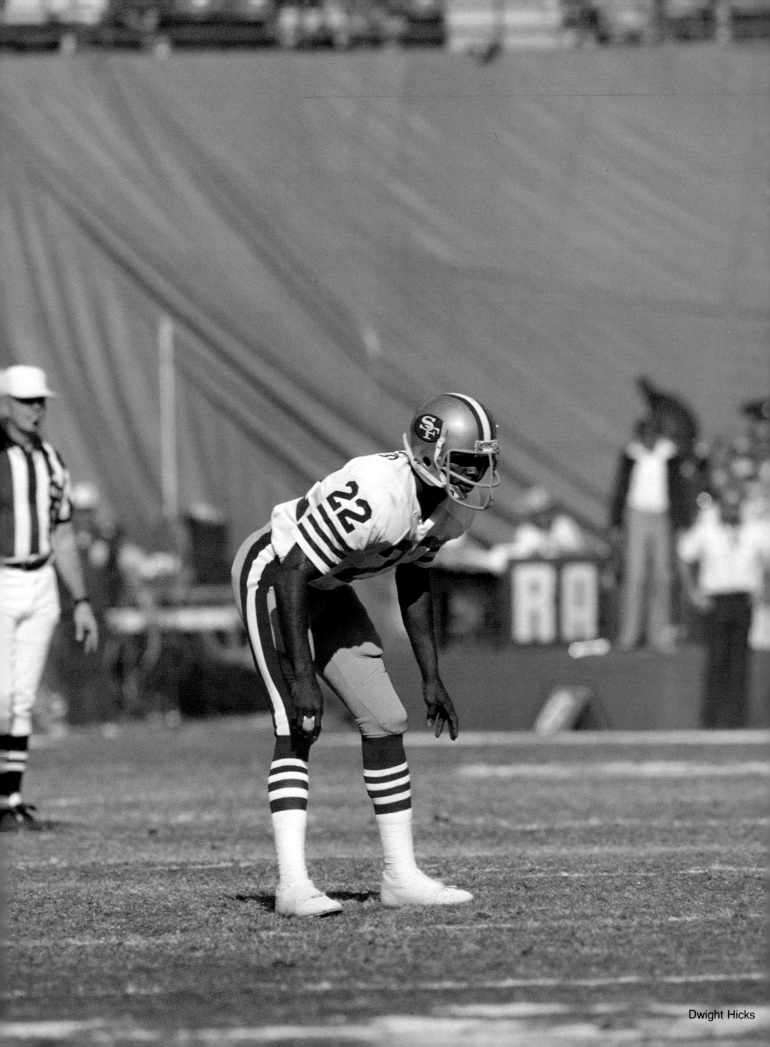

Dwight Hicks

Ronnie Lott

Ray Wersching

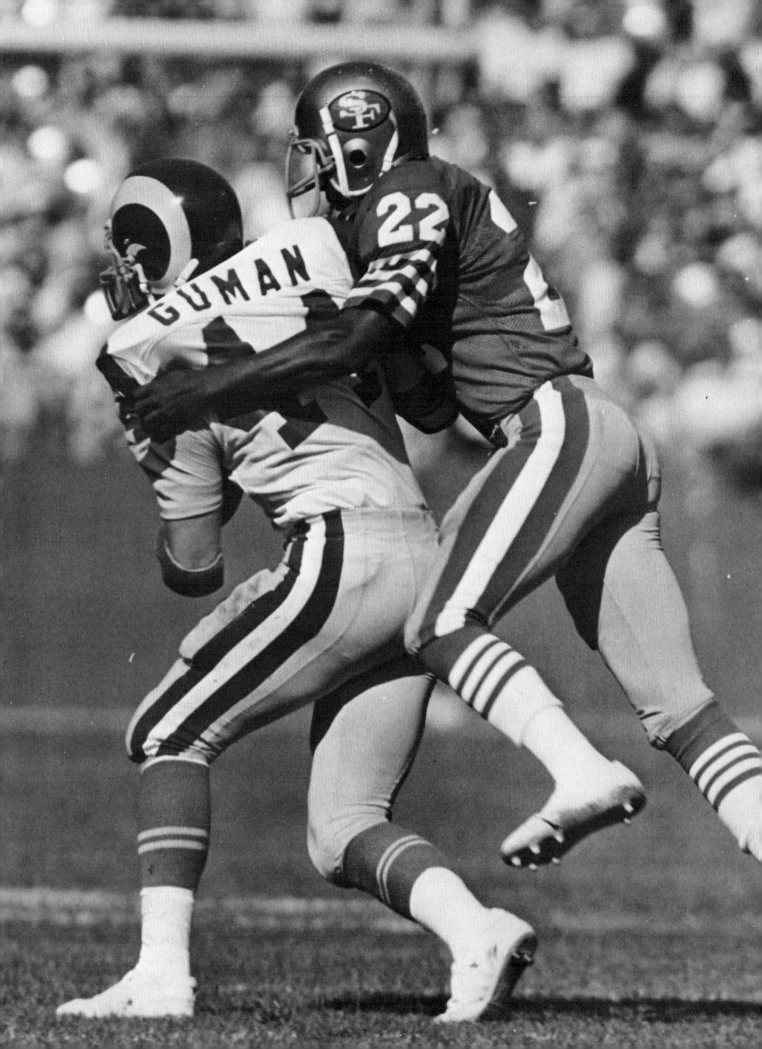

wrong way or a back cheating up. I think the coaches roomed me with Jack because they want me to become another J.R. I'm indebted to them for that.

"We both went to Tennessee; we both are self-made athletes and we both take small steps like Clydesdales. And we both are linebackers. Jack often appears gruff to outsiders, but underneath that gruff exterior is a real gentle person. It's all show. He's a very nice, warm human being."

That left Dan Bunz, the only other linebacker with appreciable experience, as a swing man. Bunz was the club's number one draft choice in 1978, and only one of four remaining draft picks from the Joe Thomas era. Besides filling in on various linebacking alignments, Bunz was an extremely valuable special teams player. At 6'4", 225 pounds, Bunz could hit.

"When I hit a guy, I don't want him to have to look up to see who hit him," Bunz said. "I want him to know."

Linebacker coach Norb Hecker knows it.

"He is very strong, very intense and he helps the team at linebacker and is a top special teams player as well," Hecker said.

The other linebacker held in reserve was Bobby Leopold. The second year veteran was drafted on the eighth round out of Notre Dame in 1980, the fourth linebacker the 49ers selected that year. At 6'1", 215 pounds, he was used on the outside behind Turner.

"Leopold is quick, active, intelligent and a relentless player," Walsh said.

The final member of the linebacking corps was Milt McColl. He is a big, 6'6", 220 pound free agent whom the 49ers signed out of Stanford in 1981 and saw action in every game during the regular season.

The key in the front line was Archie Reese. As the nose tackle on the three-man line, Reese had to exert pressure on the opposing team's center on every play. Often, he would face the challenge of two blockers. The 6'3", 262-pound Reese anchored the line after having played end in his first few years with the club. He joined the 49ers as a fifth round draft choice out of Clemson in 1978, and had practically gone unnoticed in those early years with such veterans around as Cedric Hardman,

Cornerback Ronnie Lott.

Cleveland Elam and Jimmy Webb. But, Reese is used to it. He experienced the same situation in college. After attending Clemson for two years, Reese made the football team as a walk-on, playing two years before he was given a scholarship.

"I had decided to pay my way for two years," Reese said. "I played with enthusiasm and just never gave up. I had to show leadership and do something extra. It's real hard for a nose tackle to be noticed, but the people who followed me for a long time know where I am. Hard work pays off. When you work as hard as I have in life, you'll find that good things have to happen to you."

"His personality draws the other players to him," Walsh said of Reese, whom he considers to be a leader.

On one side of Reese is Dwaine Board. The 6'5", 250-pound end was signed as a free agent in 1979, after lasting until the final cuts that year with the Pittsburgh Steelers who had drafted him on the fifth round. The Niners quickly signed him. Board made a remarkable adjustment from a small college linebacker to

...cks makes the stop on Rams' Mike Guman.

Lott intently eyes Cincinnati wide receiver Isaac Curtis.

a pro defensive end. He did so by leading the 49ers in sacks with seven, a quarter of the team's total.

"I think with a full year of experience Board can become one of the better defensive ends in pro football," Studley said. "He is fast, aggressive and has good strength-size ratio."

Unfortunately, Board lost an entire season. In the third game of the 1980 campaign, he went down with a knee injury and was finished. There was a bit of uncertainty regarding his knee when he returned for the 1981 campaign. It didn't take him long to pick up where he left off. He accounted for seven sacks again.

"I was able to come to San Francisco at a time when I had an opportunity to play," Board said. "It is tough breaking into the lineup that had been established in Pittsburgh.

With San Francisco, there were plenty of opportunities. With my training with the Steelers, everything came easier. You can sense what can happen sometimes before it happens. I had no fears. I left the Steeler camp with more confidence than I came in with."

Obtaining Fred Dean early in the season had a profound effect on Board. His sacking power diminished slightly and justifiably so.

"Fred made it tougher for me to make sacks," Board said. "My strength is speed, and getting to the quarterback, but Fred always beats me there. It's almost like a footrace. Since we got him, he always seems to win. I think our whole defense is better and the big reason is our secondary. The three rookies are excellent and they make our job more easy on the line."

Cornerback Eric Wright.

Which was fine with Jim Stuckey, the other defensive end. Drafted out of Clemson in the first round of the 1980 draft, Stuckey hadn't anticipated playing very much his rookie season. However, when Board suffered his injury, the 6'4", 251-pound Stuckey took over. He really hadn't expected it.

"I was thrust into a role that I had hoped to come into gradually," Stuckey said. "I had to perform and I know I did the best I could under the circumstances. I had to grow up fast. After I started rushing the passer in training camp, I found out I was at point zero, that I had, maybe, the physical talents, but nowhere near the technique I needed to rush the passer. I had very, very limited, basic skills.

"I don't know for sure whether the average fan understands that it takes a while to adjust in this league. I think sometimes people think a first round pick should be an NFL star right away. I think if you know how to run, like a receiver or a running back, that's the easiest thing to come into the NFL with. You've just got to learn plays. People can't teach you how to run. Being an offensive lineman or a defensive lineman, I think, is very hard. I'm coming in, doing something I've never had to do. You can be taught the techniques, but it's a long, drawn out process."

On the other hand, Lawrence Pillers made it to the 49ers, literally, overnight. The 6'4", 260-pound "super sub" played against San Francisco as a member of the New York Jets in the third game of the 1980 season. A day later, he was waived and picked up by the 49ers. He reported on a Thursday and on that Sunday he was in the starting lineup. A defensive end with the Jets, the 49ers used Pillers as a tackle

Defensive tackle Lawrence Pillers.

Defensive tackle Archie Reese.

Defensive tackle John Harty.

Defensive end Dwaine Board

when they reverted to a four man line in obvious passing situations.

"I really like playing tackle in the 4-3," Pillers said. "People say you have more freedom on the outside at end, but you also have containment responsibilities. At tackle you just go for it. I love to tee off. Our secret is hard work, determination and the addition of guys like Fred Dean, Jack Reynolds and Ronnie Lott. They're winners and it's rubbed off. We love these guys. They're good and they make us better.

"We're a hard-hitting defensive team. We go for the ball. We've got good players and a great environment. We have a lot of respect for each other. No one thinks he's better than anyone else on the team. We go through all the hard work together. Our team is a close one."

Piller's versatility enables the 49ers to make adjustments on defense. He can play all three spots on the three-man line or tackle on the four-man front. If need be, he could play end, too.

"He's really important to us," said Bill McPherson, the defensive line coach. "Like the Yankees have Goose Gossage. Pillers is our Gossage. He's accepted that role and done a great job for us. You couldn't do what we do with him with a lot of other guys. Some guys would have to change their stance, to move to the other side of the line or another position. He just goes over and does it."

Perhaps John Harty is best remembered as the other player taken in the 1981 draft besides the four defensive backs. The 6'4", 253-pound tackle was taken on the second round out of Iowa. He played primarily behind Reese and started to see more action toward the end of the season.

When the 49ers drafted Jim Miller on the third round in the 1980 draft, Walsh was elated. Miller was the first punter selected. Walsh was satisfied that he'd solved the team's punting problem for the next decade. That's how sure he was about Miller, who was the 49ers' fourth punter in four years.

Miller did his college kicking at Mississippi. The one thing everybody remembered about him there was that he kicked bare-footed and once kicked the ball off the scoreboard gon-

dola at the Superdome in New Orleans. In fact, he had been kicking that way since he was nine, growing up in Ripley, Mississippi. He wouldn't dream of putting on a shoe.

"I've got a better feel for the ball," Miller explained. "On a rainy day, your shoe is going to get real wet and heavy. I don't have any problem then. I just take a towel and wipe my foot off. I know I get the ball much higher and about 20 yards longer without a shoe. With a shoe on, there's more weight to swing and I can't get the same thrust from my leg."

Miller had difficulty the first few games of his rookie season. What it boiled down to was pressure.

"In practice, I can hit 'em all day out there," said Miller. "I'm not pressuring myself in practice. In games, I get tensed up, my legs feel real heavy."

Miller's punting woes were serious enough to alarm Walsh, who sent for punting instructor Ray Pelfray in Reno, Nevada, of all places. If there were any corrections to be made, he wanted an expert's advice.

"Punters tend to do things more comfortably in practice," Pelfray said. "In a game, by nature, they do things a little faster; and when they do that, their flaws are magnified. That's the difference between a good punt and a bad punt. The first thing a punter has to understand is the mechanics."

Miller wasn't worried. He felt good physically; he wasn't depressed.

"There's nothing to change," Miller said. "The only thing is, in a game, I'm not relaxed enough. If I was out there in practice shanking every one of 'em, I'd like some help. But maybe Pelfrey knows something. Maybe he can tell me how to relax."

Whatever happened worked. Miller finished his first season with a 40.9 average. In 1981, he was even better—41.5, kicking 16 more times in the process. Because of his high hang time, none of his punts were run back for a touchdown.

"He hasn't improved his ability to kick the ball, but it was the poise under pressure," Walsh said. "Jim got in the habit of hurrying the punt. Even when there was no pressure. It would break his timing down."

San Francisco was, at last, a complete team.

THE 1981 SEASON

Their optimism was guarded as the 49ers reported to training camp to prepare for the 1981 season. The year before, San Francisco had finished the 1980 campaign with a modest 6-10 record—not exactly a performance on which to build championship dreams. That year the 49ers had had a euphoric beginning, winning their first three games. Then they'd lost eight consecutive games, and it seemed as if they had reverted back to being the same old losers. Then again, they won three straight games, only to lose their two final contests and any chance of a .500 season.

Nevertheless, Walsh knew that San Francisco could achieve a successful season in 1981. He had seen some positive developments during the 1980 season, and these were substantiated by the game films, which he spent long hours reviewing before training camp opened. He also detected a general sense of stability in his club, despite the fact that the 49ers had barely recovered from the trades for Jim Plunkett in 1976 and O.J. Simpson in 1978. At the time, those trades had depleted their draft selections, and convinced Walsh that it would take three or four drafts for the 49ers to achieve the competitive level required for the playoffs.

Walsh approached the 1981 draft brashly. The 1980 crop of college players was loaded with quality defensive backs. (What better time to repair a leaky roof?) Instead of picking one, Walsh amazed the pro football establishment by grabbing three defensive backs in his first four picks. He took still another on the fifth round. No one could remember when anyone had used 80% of their resources in a single area like this before.

In late June, Walsh augmented his drive by signing veteran linebacker Jack Reynolds as a free agent.

What the 49ers' offense had accomplished during the 1980 season pleased him. They had finished seventh in the National Football Conference on offense, yet third in passing statistics. However, on defense they ranked 13th, having yielded only one less point than the year before, 415. It was no wonder that defense was his prime area of concern.

"We are seeking a reservoir of defensive talent, talent that can deal with the multi-faceted offense we face in the NFL today," Walsh explained. "We need overall defensive improvement and we need improved personnel. The days of a great NFL team relying on eight

101

or nine great defensive players from that unit are gone. Today a pool of 18 solid defensive players, starters and capable backups, is needed to win. And we still have a distance to travel before we can meet those requirements."

The 49ers had to establish a defensive personality. In 1980, they began the season playing the 4-3. Midway through the campaign, they switched and incorporated the 3-4 into their defensive scheme. They performed better with that alignment. Before utilizing the 3-4, the defense had yielded an average of 31.6 points a game—hardly playoff form. Adopting the 3-4, the defense permitted an average of only 20.3 points. It was a significant difference; not quite championship caliber but close nevertheless.

As far as the offense was concerned Walsh was satisfied, although he insisted that the 49ers had to score more. He was convinced he had a solid young quarterback in Joe Montana, whom he had drafted in 1979. Montana played very little his first year, and shared much of the playing with Steve DeBerg the following season. But, not an advocate of a two-quarterback system, by August of 1981, Walsh had traded DeBerg to Denver despite the fact that he was more experienced than Montana and had set an NFL record in completions and passes attempted in 1979. Walsh saw that Montana had a knack for making things happen and withstood pressure better than DeBerg. Furthermore, Montana was the first 49er quarterback to throw more touchdowns than interceptions since Steve Spurrier in 1972.

"Joe is intelligent and quick on his feet," said Walsh at the outset of the season. "He improved weekly as he began getting into the starting role. We expect more improvement from him in 1981. He had the highest completion percentage in the NFL last year, and the best in 49er history, at 64.5, and had the lowest interception percentage in the league at 3.3. People said he was inconsistent at Notre Dame. But looking back, I think it may have been the system they were operating because he hasn't been inconsistent here."

As Walsh started his third season, only a handful of the players that had been with the

team when he took over in 1979, remained. They included: linebackers Willie Harper and Dan Bunz, running back Paul Hofer, guards John Ayers, Randy Cross and Walt Downing, center Fred Quillan, tackle Keith Fahnhorst, defensive tackle Archie Reese, wide receiver Fred Solomon and kicker Ray Wersching.

Even so, the 49ers weren't taken seriously before the 1981 season began. They were picked to finish no higher than third in the Western Division. (Some thought they would finish last.) Atlanta was the heavy favorite, followed by Los Angeles, with a battle between

Charle Young is about to be brought down after catching a pass.

San Francisco and New Orleans for third place. The analysts pointed to a number of reasons why the 49ers would have to struggle even to reach .500.

• Defensive end Dwaine Board was coming off knee surgery.

• The 49er running game was suspect, accented by the fact that running back Paul Hofer was recuperating from a major knee operation. Without Hofer, San Francisco's short passing game suffered noticeably.

• San Francisco was still trying to construct a formidable defense with either a 4-3 or a 3-4

allignment.

• It wasn't known if Montana could hold up all season as the starting quarterback.

• The 49er secondary would probably be weak with four untested rookies.

• It didn't look as though Dan Audick would help on the offensive line.

Walsh scoffed at his critics.

"We've established a very positive, confident atmosphere in the organization, especially among the players," he said. "When I was hired, one of the most difficult hurdles was the team's low motivation. I feel the current

Walt Easley just makes it across the goal line.

mood has overcome that. We've become competitive, psychologically and emotionally."

As training camp began, Walsh was certain of a .500 season. Before it was over, he was thinking in terms of a 9-7 record with a possible wild card entry into the playoffs if Atlanta and Los Angeles stumbled. Before mid-season he'd signed defensive end Fred Dean, in a decisive move for the playoffs. Dean provided the missing link. Since he'd come into the picture, the 49ers had won ten out of eleven games and fooled everyone by winning the Western Division championship.

GAME ONE: DETROIT

The first test of Walsh's optimism—and Montana's position as the 49ers' established quarterback—was set for a road opening in Detroit. The Lions had playoff aspirations of their own, primarily because of the running ability of Billy Sims. As a rookie the year before, Sims led the NFL in touchdowns with 16 and set a Lion rushing record with 1,303 yards. Coupled with Gary Danielson's passing, and a better-than-average defense, the Lions had finished 1980 with 9-7 record and high hopes for 1981.

The Lions took the opening kickoff of the season and it looked like they would score a touchdown on their initial drive. Starting on their 26 yard line, they drove to the 49ers' 25 yard line before stalling. At that point Ed Murray's 42-yard field goal attempt failed. However, San Francisco's offense sputtered during the first period. The Niners advanced only 15 yards the first time they got the ball. Then, after Willie Harper recovered Sims' fumble on the 49ers' 15 yard line, San Francisco managed to get to midfield before the quarter ended.

The 49ers succeeded in scoring the game's first points. With about five minutes left in the half, Wersching booted a 25-yard field goal to culminate a modest drive that had begun on Detroit's 44 yard line. Then, just when it looked like the 49ers would wind up their first half efforts with a 3-0 lead, the Lions struck twice in two minutes. First, Danielson hit Sims with a 39-yard touchdown pass to give Detroit a 7-3 lead. When Ray Jones fumbled the kickoff on the 25 yard line, Detroit had another scoring opportunity. Only one second remained when Murray kicked a 29-yard field goal to provide the lions with 10-3 halftime advantage.

The 49ers took the second half kickoff and put together a good-looking drive. Montana completed all four passes he threw as the 49ers went from their own 23 yard line to Detroit's 15, where they were stopped. They still had a chance to score, but Wersching's 32-yard field goal attempt sailed wide to the right.

San Francisco's defense hung tough. They yielded only one first down and forced the Lions to punt. With 7:22 left in the quarter, San Francisco dominated the action the rest of the period. Starting on their own 45 yard line, the 49ers drove to the Lions' one yard line before time ran out. On the first play of the fourth quarter, Ricky Patton dove into the middle for the tying touchdown.

Detroit answered back. They drove 64 yards in nine plays to regain the lead, 17-10. This time the touchdown was the result of a breakdown in the 49ers' young secondary, which allowed Danielson to loft a 17-yard pass to his running back, Horace King, who was all alone in the end zone.

The 49ers wouldn't quit. With Patton leading the way, they marched 74 yards in just seven plays. Patton displayed fine form, running for 15 and 22 yards. Montana hooked up with Solomon for the tying touchdown with a well-thrown 21-yard pass between two defenders, deadlocking the contest at 17-17. Unfortunately, that was their last offensive thrust of the day. Moving from midfield, Detroit punched over the winning touchdown when Sims dove into the end zone from the one yard line. Detroit had a 24-17 victory.

"Our kickoff killed us," Walsh said. "Ray Wersching pulled a muscle in his leg in the pre-game warmups and we had problems the whole game. The kicking game allowed the Lions good field position. I knew we were in trouble, even on extra points. Our defense is going to come of age. They're young players and they played extremely well. We sputtered quite a bit offensively."

San Francisco	0	3	0	14	17
Detroit	0	10	0	14	24

San Francisco: 10:32, second period—Wersching 25-yard field goal.
Detroit: 14:32, second period—Sims 39-yard pass from Danielson (Murray, kick)
Detroit: 15:00, second period—Murray 29-yard field goal
San Francisco: 9:06, fourth period—Patton 1-yard run (Wersching, kick)
Detroit: 4:29, fourth period—King 17-yard pass from Danielson (Murray, kick)
San Francisco: 7:30, fourth period—Solomon 21-yard pass from Montana (Wersching, kick)
Detroit: 14:42, fourth period—Sims 1-yard run (Murray, kick)

GAME TWO: CHICAGO

A crowd of 49,520 came out to Candlestick Park to see the new-look 49ers in their home opener. For the second straight week, San Francisco faced an NFC Central Division opponent in the Chicago Bears. The Bears had also lost their opening game of the season, bowing to the Green Bay Packers, 16-9. Although they had quarterback problems, the presence of their star runner Walter Payton, and a good defense, made the Bears dangerous.

105

Montana didn't seem too sharp the first time San Francisco got the ball. He missed on the first three passes. However, the third time the 49ers got the ball, Montana led them on a 70-yard drive in only six plays, completing all three passes he threw. The payoff was a 31-yard touchdown pass to Patton that gave the 49ers a 7-0 lead some five minutes before the first period ended.

Just three minutes after play began in the second quarter, Montana hooked up with Solomon on a well-timed play for a 46-yard touchdown pass. When Matt Bahr, replacing the injured Wersching, converted for the second time, San Francisco moved into a 14-0 lead.

The 49ers seemed to be in command. However, the next time they had the ball, they allowed the Bears to get back into the game. Center Bill Quillan's snap went right through Montana's legs as he was set on the 23 yard line, and the ball rolled all the way back to the four yard line where Mike Hartenstine recovered for the Bears. Two plays later, Payton went in for a touchdown that cut San Francisco's lead in half, 14-7.

The next time the Bears got the ball, with only 35 seconds remaining in the half, they scored again after linebacker Keena Turner almost intercepted quarterback Vince Evans' third down pass, and Bob Thomas came in to kick a 37-yard field goal. San Francisco's margin was narrowed to 14-10 at intermission.

Chicago continued to roll when play resumed. They took the second half kickoff and drove 68 yards in ten plays. The touchdown came in a five-yard pass from Evans to tight end Robin Earl. They took over the lead, 17-14. The 49ers, who had started out with a 14-0 lead, now found themselves behind.

A turnover gave the 49ers an opportunity to come back when, in a rare moment, Payton fumbled and linebacker Dan Bunz recovered for the Niners on the Chicago 33 yard line. It didn't take Montana long to get San Francisco back in front. He first passed to Solomon for 28 yards and then quickly hit tight end Charle Young with a four-yard touchdown pass that restored San Francisco's lead, 21-17.

When the third period ended, the Bears had a drive going that had reached San Francisco's 23 yard line. Within the first few minutes of the fourth quarter they were on the two yard line, primed to score. However, Payton, who had made only two fumbles the entire 1980 season, fumbled for the second time when hit hard by Bunz. Craig Puki pounced on the ball to turn the Bears back.

San Francisco got the clinching touchdown with just 1:31 left in the game. Following a block by guard Randy Cross, Patton swept around right end from the 12 yard line to stretch the 49ers' lead to 28-17 and insure the team's first win of the season.

Montana had given 49er fans a hint of what was to come. And he'd enjoyed the finest game of his career to date, completing 20 of 32 passes for 287 yards and three touchdowns.

Chicago	0	10	7	0	17
San Francisco	7	7	7	7	28

San Francisco: 9:37, first period—Patton 31-yard pass from Montana (Bahr, kick)
San Francisco: 3:08, second period—Solomon 46-yard pass from Montana (Bahr, kick)
Chicago: 8:33, second period—Payton 2-yard run (Thomas, kick)
Chicago: 14:28, second period—Thomas 37-yard field goal
Chicago: 3:24, third period—Earl 12-yard pass from Evans (Thomas, kick)
San Francisco: 9:19, third period—Young 5-yard pass from Montana (Bahr, kick)
San Francisco: 13:35, fourth period—Patton 12-yard run (Bahr, kick)

GAME THREE: ATLANTA

Early season games are not generally regarded as crucial in a 16-game schedule. There was no denying the fact, however, that San Francisco was facing a major confrontation when they met the Atlanta Falcons in Atlanta the third week of the campaign. The Falcons were picked by the experts to win the Western Division championship and to continue their flight to the Super Bowl. By that time Atlanta had already trounced New Orleans, 27-0, and erupted for 31 points in the fourth quarter to stun Green Bay, 31-17, the following week.

Atlanta quarterback Steve Bartkowski had been impressive, even though he was suffering from a cracked rib, passing for four touchdowns in the first two games. A strong-

Eason Ramson looks for a pass from Joe Montana.

armed veteran, he represented a real test for the 49ers' unseasoned secondary. Bartkowski was also supported by a strong running attack that included William Andrews and Lynn Cain.

After receiving the opening kickoff, Bartkowski picked up where he'd left off the previous week. He completed a seven-play, 72-yard drive with a 29-yard touchdown pass to Alfred Jackson for the Falcons' first touchdown. After stopping the 49ers in their first series, Bartkowski got the Falcons close enough for a 47-yard field goal by rookie Mick Luckhurst to make the score 10-0.

San Francisco couldn't get untracked. Ronnie Lott fumbled the kickoff, and the Falcons had another scoring opportunity on the 21 yard line. Three plays later, Bartkowski fired an 18-yard touchdown pass to Cain and sent the Falcons into a 17-0 lead as the first period came to a close.

In the opening minutes of the second quarter, Montana got the Niners on the scoreboard. He led them on a nine-play, 80-yard drive, finishing it with a quick seven-yard touchdown pass to Young. Bahr's conversion made the score 17-7. Minutes later, Bahr contributed a 47-yard field goal to bring the 49ers closer at 17-10.

Atlanta answered back. They took the kickoff and marched 80 yards in ten plays. Bartkowski provided the touchdown with his third scoring pass of the game, a 15-yard strike to wide receiver Al Jenkins that upped Atlanta's advantage to 24-10. The 49ers' furious effort to score before the half ended was thwarted when Bahr's 24-yard field goal attempt was blocked.

The 49ers started out smartly in the second half. They drove from their own 27 yard line to the Altlanta six, where Montana faced a third down. He called Young's number but free safety Tom Pridemore was waiting. He intercepted Montana's pass one yard into the end zone and ran it back for a club record of 101 yards and a touchdown for the Falcons. That play ignited the crowd but stunned the 49ers, who fell behind 31-10. Atlanta added to its lead the next time they had the ball, when Luckhurst kicked an 18-yard field goal, extending the Falcons' bulge to 34-10.

The Niners would never be able to come back in the fourth quarter. Nevertheless, Montana directed them on a 77-yard drive that took only seven plays, the final one a 12-yard touchdown pass to Solomon that reduced Atlanta's margin of victory to 34-17. Defensive coordinator Chuck Studley wasn't pleased with the way his unit had played.

"It looked like every time we went to make a tackle, everybody else stopped pursuing," he said.

"They look like they are ready to make a real bid for the Super Bowl," said Walsh, in appraising the Falcons. "They are an outstanding team. We misfired with early mistakes and they took advantage."

San Francisco	0	10	0	7	17
Atlanta	17	7	10	0	34

Atlanta: 3:39, first period—Jackson 29-yard pass from Bartkowski (Luckhurst, kick)
Atlanta: 9:46, first period—Luckhurst 47-yard field goal
Atlanta: 11:03, first period—Cain 18-yard pass from Bartkowski (Luckhurst, kick)
San Francisco: 1:28, second period—Young 11-yard pass from Montana (Bahr, kick)
San Francisco: 6:05, second period—Bahr 47-yard field goal
Atlanta: 10:03, second period—Jenkins 15-yard pass from Bartkowski (Luckhurst, kick)
Atlanta: 5:21, third period—Pridemore 101-yard interception return (Luckhurst, kick)
Atlanta: 10:56, third period—Luckhurst 18-yard field goal
San Francisco: 8:50, fourth period—Solomon 12-yard pass from Montana (Bahr, kick)

GAME FOUR: NEW ORLEANS

When the 49ers returned home to face the New Orleans Saints after a 1-2 beginning, the pessimists were starting to talk about another losing season. It reflected in attendance. Only 44,433 showed up on a comfortable afternoon when the temperature hit 68—5,000 fewer fans than on opening day two weeks before.

The Saints were also 1-2. They, too, had lost their opening game and had rebounded to upset Los Angeles, only to lose to the New York Giants. They'd been beaten by Atlanta 27-0 on the very first day of the season, in Coach Bum Phillips' debut in the NFC.

Most of New Orleans' offense was generated by the combined efforts of quarterback Archie Manning and speedy wide receiver Wes Chandler, augmented by running back

Willie Harper makes a powerful charge against the Saints.

George Rogers (the first player selected in the 1981 college draft). Manning wasn't expected to start against the Niners because he'd injured his hamstring against Los Angeles and didn't play against the Giants. That meant that the 49ers would have to face rookie Dave Wilson. Paul Hofer was expecting to see a lot of action for the 49ers.

The first three times the 49ers had the ball on offense, they didn't do much with it. In fact, they never even crossed midfield. The closest they came was to the 49 yard line on their first series before they punted. An interception stopped them the second time, and they were forced to punt the third time. The Saints scored first. They did so on an 80-yard drive in just seven plays. The big play of the series was a 39-yard reception by Chandler. Then Wilson got the touchdown with a 24-yard pass to his other wide receiver, Jeff Groth, to give the Saints a 7-0 lead with just 1:37 left in the quarter.

Mixing his plays well, Montana got the 49ers moving after that. In a drive that began in the closing minutes of the first period, he led the Niners 69 yards in 15 plays for the tying touchdown. The drive consumed 6:35 with Johnny Davis scoring the touchdown on a six-yard run off the right side.

Neither team could do much after that. The only serious scoring threat was produced by New Orleans with just over a minute left in the first half. They started a drive on their own 27 yard line and reached the 49ers' six yard line before faltering. The Saints tried a field goal with time running out but holder Tom Myers fumbled the snap. The teams went into the dressing rooms deadlocked at 7-7.

In their first chance on offense in the third quarter, the 49ers scored suddenly in one play. New Orleans had punted to the San Francisco 38 yard line after failing to advance, and Patton managed a couple of yards before Montana and Solomon brought the crowd to its feet. Montana completed a pass to his swift wide receiver on the New Orleans 35 yard line. With that Solomon bounced off a defender and ran the rest of the way into the end zone. Bahr added the conversion to give San Francisco a 14-7 lead. From there, the 49er defense took over and stopped the Saints for

the remainder of the quarter.

Early in the fourth period, the defense contributed to the score as Manning entered the game for the first time. When his second pass went through Chandler's hands, Lott intercepted and ran 26 yards for a touchdown—the first of his pro career. Bahr's kick made it 21-7.

There was no flaw in Manning's arm the last time the Saints got the ball. In a 14-play drive that covered 80 yards, he threw 12 passes, the final one finding Wayne Wilson for a nine-yard touchdown that reduced San Francisco's winning margin to 21-14.

"We didn't move the ball as we normally do, but you have to give credit to the Saints for that," Walsh said afterward. "We got conservative because we figured mistakes could beat us. Our defensive backs have great talent; they have the whole future ahead of them."

New Orleans		7	0	0	7	14
San Francisco		0	7	7	7	21

New Orleans:13:23, first period—Groth 24-yard pass from D. Wilson (Ricardo, kick)
San Francisco: 5:08, second period—Davis 6-yard run (Bahr, kick)
San Francisco: 3:12, third period—Solomon 60-yard pass from Montana (Bahr, kick)
San Francisco: 3:28, fourth period—Lott 26-yard interception return (Bahr, kick)
New Orleans: 13:51, fourth period—W. Wilson 9-yard pass from Manning (Ricardo, kick)

GAME FIVE: WASHINGTON

Even though they had split their first four games, the 49ers were only one game out of first place. While they'd been defeating New Orleans, the Cleveland Browns had upended Atlanta to knock them from the unbeaten ranks and tighten the Western Conference race.

Walsh and his players realized they had a good opportunity to remain near the top of the conference battle. Now, in the fifth week of the campaign, they faced the Redskins in Washington. Under new coach Joe Gibbs, the Redskins were having trouble. They had lost all four games of the season. However, the Niners knew about losing on the road. In the past 28 times they played away, they'd lost 26 times.

Fred Solomon makes a spectacular over the shoulder catch in Redskin game.

Charle Young tries to break away from Dallas safety Charlie Waters.

The 49ers took the opening kickoff and marched straight down the field. Balancing his plays nicely, Montana directed the Niners on an 80-yard drive that took 13 plays and used up 5:38 on the clock. Then Patton slipped through the Washington defense for a 16-yard touchdown run, and Bahr's kick made it 7-0.

It was the defense's turn to score and they did so dramatically. The Redskins had reached the 49ers' 22 yard line in their struggle to tie the game. On first down, Ronnie Lott knocked the ball loose from Terry Metcalf when he'd reached the 20. Dwight Hicks caught the loose ball in the air and ran 80 yards untouched for a touchdown to give the 49ers a 14-0 lead when the quarter ended.

Early in the second quarter, Bahr booted a 43-yard field goal that stretched San Francisco's margin to 17-0. Washington scored next as Mark Moseley kicked a 34-yard field goal to get the Redskins on the board at 17-3.

The Niners came right back to extend their lead. In seven plays, Montana took the 49ers 64 yards, opening the drive with a 40-yard pass completion to Solomon and ending with

Johnny Davis cracking over from the one yard line. When the half ended, San Francisco was ahead, 24-3.

Later, with six minutes left in the third period, the San Francisco defense struck again. This time, Dwight Hicks picked off a pass by Joe Theismann and raced 32 yards for a touchdown that sent the 49ers soaring into a 30-3 lead. After Bahr's conversion attempt failed, the frustrated Theismann was relieved by Tom Flick.

A good part of the crowd of 51,843 started to leave RFK Stadium when the fourth period began. At that point the outcome was inevitable and all they missed were a couple of meaningless Washington touchdowns. The first was a 53-yard punt return by Mike Nelms that reduced San Francisco's margin to 30-10. the The other was set up by Montana's only interception, on the 49er 30 yard line. Joe Washington carried the final five yards for the touchdown that put the final score at 30-17.

The 49ers' secondary was coming of age. Hicks had outgained everyone on the field with a total of 184 return yards on two interceptions and a fumble recovery. It was a complete victory, offensively and defensively.

"I think we have some good, talented young players on defense," said Walsh after the game. "Our young players have outstanding futures. Hicks is becoming one of the great free safeties in football. I don't know if there is a better safety in football. Our quarterback played well and didn't let himself get into trouble. We had planned to throw the ball and in the first half we were successful; in the second half we let up.

| San Francisco | 14 | 10 | 6 | 0 | 30 |
| Washington | 0 | 3 | 0 | 14 | 17 |

San Francisco: 5:38, first period—Patton 76-yard run (Bahr, kick)
San Francisco: 10:44, first period—Hicks 80-yard fumble return (Bahr, kick)
San Francisco: 2:38, second period—Bahr 43-yard field goal
Washington: 6:14, second period—Moseley 34-yard field goal
San Francisco: 8:43, third period—Davis 1-yard run (Bahr, kick)
San Francisco: 9:09, third period—Hicks 32-yard interception return (kick failed)
Washington: 4:27, fourth period—Nelms 53-yard punt return (Moseley, kick)

GAME SIX: DALLAS

San Francisco was now sharing first place with Atlanta and Los Angeles. All three teams had 3-2 records, and suddenly there was a legitimate race on after the experts had all but conceded the divisional title to the Falcons (who by now had lost two consecutive games).

If the Niners had any serious title claim, it would be challenged when they returned home to meet the Dallas Cowboys, the one team most often picked to win the NFC championship. The Cowboys had won their first four games before stumbling to their first loss against St. Louis, 20-17. No one gave the 49ers a second thought at this point.

However, Walsh made some significant changes before the game. The biggest was signing defensive end Fred Dean, who had left the San Diego Chargers in a contract dispute. The other was restoring Ray Wersching to the active roster after he'd been sidelined for a month. A crowd of 57,574 turned out to see if the 49ers could contain Danny White's passing and Tony Dorsett's running while overcoming Dallas' strong defense.

San Francisco took the opening kickoff and went 61 yards in 11 plays. The payoff was a quick one-yard pass from Montana to Solomon for a touchdown. Wersching's kick made it 7-0. The next time the 49ers got the ball, they scored again. This time they went 68 yards in just eight plays. Paul Hofer, testing his injured knee, scored the touchdown on a four-yard run, to give the Niners a 14-0 advantage.

The offense wasn't having any trouble moving the ball and the San Francisco defense was in control. They rejected the Cowboys' efforts to produce a first down the first three times they had the ball. Then, less than two minutes from the conclusion of the quarter, the 49ers stunned the Cowboys a third time, when Lott recovered a Dallas fumble on the Cowboys' six yard line. On fourth down and one, San Francisco elected to go for the touchdown instead of a sure field goal. Johnny Davis plunged into the end zone, and sent the 49ers into a 21-0 lead.

Only 57 seconds remained when San Francisco again got the ball in Dallas territory. Lott intercepted White's pass and returned it 12 yards to the 33 yard line. Three plays later, as the quarter ended, the 49ers had reached the five yard stripe. Shortly after the second period began, the 49ers reached the one. This time on fourth down they settled for Wersching's 18-yard field goal. San Francisco's lead ballooned to 24-0.

Frustrated, the Cowboys finally scored with about four minutes left in the one-sided half, using a trick play. White flipped a lateral to tight end Billy Joe DuPree, who threw a 22-yard touchdown pass to Tony Hill. But the 49ers were still in command at intermission, 24-7.

The Cowboys may have had comeback hopes in the third period, but Montana and Clark, collaborating on a 78-yard touchdown pass, squelched them as the 49ers stretched their advantage to 31-7. Right after that, Lott intercepted White's pass from the shotgun formation and returned it for a 41-yard touchdown that sent San Francisco soaring, 38-7. And the 49ers weren't finished. Completing a drive that began near the end of the third period, they scored after two minutes had elapsed in the final quarter. Amos Lawrence scored on a one-yard run, the 16th play in an 89-yard drive that had consumed 9:28. It seemed like eternity to Dallas. It didn't matter that Benny Barnes ran back a fumble 72 yards for a touchdown. The Cowboys were thoroughly humiliated, 45-14.

"This win was very gratifying for us," said Walsh. "We tried to prove to doubters that we have a competitive team. We know we've been playing well despite what you read in the press. The key is that we're maturing."

Dallas	0	7	0	7	14
San Francisco	21	3	14	7	45

San Francisco: 3:45, first period—Solomon 1-yard pass from Montana (Wersching, kick)
San Francisco: 7:53, first period—Hofer 4-yard run (Wersching, kick)
San Francisco: 13:46, first period—Davis 1-yard run (Wersching, kick)
San Francisco: 1:26, second period—Wersching 18-yard field goal
Dallas: 11:01, second period—Hill 22-yard pass from DuPree (Septien, kick)
San Francisco: 5:48, third period—Clark 78-yard pass from Montana (Wersching, kick)
San Francisco: 6:23, third period—Lott 41-yard interception return (Wersching, kick)
San Francisco: 2:07, fourth period—Lawrence 1-yard run (Wersching, kick)
Dallas: 6:53, fourth period—Barnes 72-yard fumble return (Septien, kick)

GAME SEVEN: GREEN BAY

They were back on the road for the fourth time in the season. This time, NFL experts took notice, and early season detractors were questioning whether or not San Francisco was a bona fide playoff possibility. Their convincing triumph over Dallas had everybody wondering.

When the 49ers arrived in Milwaukee for their game against Green Bay, they were still tied for first place with a 4-2 record. Atlanta had fallen for the third straight week in a wild scoring contest where the Rams had edged the Falcons, 37-35, to push them into second place with a 3-3 record. San Francisco shared the top spot with Los Angeles.

Green Bay coach Bart Starr was feeling the pressure of a losing season. The Packers were 2-4 and there were rumors that his job was in jeopardy. Nonetheless, the 49ers had to be wary of the Pack simply because they possessed two of the swiftest wide receivers in the NFL—John Jefferson and James Lofton. It was typical Wisconsin weather for late October—windy with a chance of snow flurries. But a crowd of 50,171 was on hand, despite the blustery forecast.

The offenses of both teams were sputtering in the first quarter. The first three times the Packers had the ball they could only produce one first down. San Francisco's efforts were equally futile. When the first period action ended, the Packers had succeeded in going from their 20 yard line to the 49er 12, behind the passing of Lynn Dickey.

Then just after the second period began, Green Bay broke through. Jan Stenerud kicked a 26-yard field goal for a 3-0 Packer lead, which held until the final seconds of the first half. Then the 49ers developed their first drive of the game, and moved from their own 20 yard line to the Green Bay nine. There Wersching tied the game with a 26-yard field goal.

Johnny Davis protects the ball heading into the Green Bay line.

Statistically, the struggle was even. Both teams had had nine first downs, the Packers had gained 150 yards while the 49ers had 149, each team had punted four times, and the 49ers had converted one of seven third down situations while Green Bay failed to achieve one in six attempts. San Francisco had had the ball for 15:06; Green Bay for 14:54. The defenses were in control.

San Francisco finally found the end zone the second time they had the ball in the third period. Starting with good field position on the Green Bay 46 yard line, the 49ers drove for the touchdown in ten plays with Johnny Davis busting over from the one on fourth down. Wersching's conversion gave the Niners a 10-3 lead as the period came to an end.

In a time-controlled drive, the 49ers put the game away in the fourth period with a 14-play offensive series that took 7:10 to complete. With a little over four minutes left in the game, Wersching booted a 32-yard field goal to set the 49ers' victory at 13-3.

In all, San Francisco's defense had been particularly impressive. They'd limited the Packers to 47 plays and a total of 241 yards, and shut them out on third down conversions in ten attempts. Lawrence Pillers had sacked Dickey three times, taking advantage of the fact that the Packers double-teamed Dean. Despite not scoring many points, the offense had managed to keep control of the ball for over 37 minutes.

"Our pass rush was trouble," Walsh said commenting on the team's performance "I thought it made the difference in the two teams. We played a tactical game."

San Francisco	0	3	7	3	13
Green Bay	0	3	0	0	3

Green Bay: 1:26, second period—Stenerud 26-yard field goal
San Francisco: 14:57, second period—Wersching 26-yard field goal
San Francisco: 11:49, third period—Davis 1-yard run (Wersching, kick)
San Francisco: 10:29, fourth period—Wersching 32-yard field goal

GAME EIGHT: LOS ANGELES

Even the biggest skeptics were aware of what was happening in San Francisco. Who would have believed that the 49ers would be leading the Western Division by one game as the season reached the halfway point? If there was a miracle in the making it would take shape on this Sunday, October 25, at Candlestick Park.

The 49ers had won four games in succession, giving them a 5-2 record. The second place Los Angeles Rams, who were to face the Niners for the first time, were 4-3. The Rams hadn't lost to San Francisco at Candlestick since the stadium opened in 1966. A crowd of 59,190 showed up to see whether the 49ers were for real.

San Francisco couldn't produce a first down the first two times they had their hands on the ball. However, on their third try, Montana led the Niners on a 68-yard offensive in nine plays. He completed five of six passes, the final being a 14-yard touchdown strike to Solomon, which got the 49ers on the board first.

The 49ers scored again the next time they went on offense. This time Montana hooked up with Clark on a 41-yard touchdown pass just one second before the quarter ended, to push San Francisco into a 14-0 lead.

Midway through the second period, the Rams broke through, though not for a touchdown. After the 49er defense stiffened three times inside the nine yard line, Los Angeles had to settle for a 25-yard field goal by Pat Corral that trimmed San Francisco's edge to 14-3.

After checking the 49ers, the Rams got the ball back with 5:58 remaining. Pat Haden led the Rams on a 96-yard march, with Mike Guman getting the final two yards for the Rams' first touchdown, pulling them within 14-10.

There were only 59 seconds left in the first half when the 49ers got the ball on the 22 yard line following the kickoff. A big second down pass play from Montana to Cooper gained them 50 yards and enabled to Niners to think about a field goal. They had just barely accomplished their mission when Wersching drilled a 42-yarder through the crossbars. Time ran out with San Francisco ahead, 17-10.

Although the Rams were behind, it wasn't obvious from the first half statistics. They'd had the ball six minutes longer than the 49ers,

Cocking his arm way back, Joe Montana is about to launch a high pass over the arms of a tall Ram lineman.

they had the edge in first downs, 13-9, they'd outgained them 240 to 179 yards, and had run off 46 plays to 30. While the 49ers had failed to convert in all four third down situations, the Rams had been successful on six of 13. The Niner defense had a job before them to keep the Rams in check.

They did so for most of the third quarter. On their second offensive possession, Montana directed them on a long march that began on the 20 yard line and reached the Ram one yard line. On the previous third down play, Montana had come up a yard short on a quarter draw play, but on fourth down, Wersching kicked an 18-yard field goal that lifted the 49ers into a 20-10 lead.

Los Angeles came back after the kickoff. Haden took them 66 yards in just five plays, culminating with a 16-yard touchdown pass to Wendell Tyler that narrowed San Francisco's lead to 20-17 just before the conclusion of the third period.

Although the 49ers didn't come close to scoring in the final period, they survived two game-tying field goal attempts by the Rams. The first came with six minutes left on the clock when Corral's 32-yard try hit the right upright. Then, with just 45 seconds left in the game, Corral's 45-yard attempt sailed wide to the left. San Francisco prevailed, 20-17. The defense, with Dean accounting for 4½ sacks, had made the difference.

"It was a tremendous victory," Walsh exclaimed. "It was the defense that picked us up in the second half when our offense was unable to sustain drives. Dean is a great player. He's obviously made a big difference."

| Los Angeles | 0 | 10 | 7 | 0 | 17 |
| San Francisco | 14 | 3 | 3 | 0 | 20 |

San Francisco: 9:38, first period—Solomon 14-yard pass from Montana (Wersching, kick)
San Francisco: 14:59, first period—Clark 41-yard pass from Montana (Wersching, kick)
Los Angeles: 7:22, second period—Corral, 25-yard field goal
Los Angeles: 13:57, second period—Guman 2-yard run (Corral, kick)
San Francisco: 15:00, second period—Wersching 42-yard field goal
San Francisco: 12:01, third period—Wersching 18-yard field goal
Los Angeles: 14:04, third period—Tyler 16-yard pass from Haden (Corral, kick)

GAME NINE: PITTSBURGH

If San Francisco was feeling a little heady it was understandable. The 1981 season was half over and the 49ers were leading the Western Division by two games. They had won five games in a row and had two teams, Los Angeles and Atlanta, chasing them. Only Philadelphia, with a 7-1 mark, had a better record. San Francisco was 6-2 and looking better every week.

The Niners had to pack their bags again, this time to meet the Pittsburgh Steelers. The

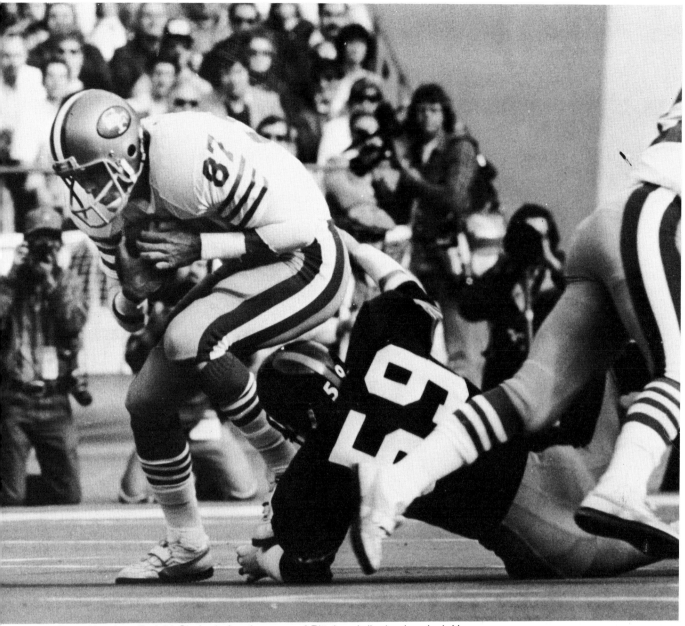

Crouching low, Dwight Clark eludes the arms of Pittsburgh linebacker Jack Ham.

Steelers, after some early season difficulties, had improved their record to 5-3. They were still a formidable contender with Terry Bradshaw, wide receivers Lynn Swann, Jim Smith and John Stallworth, running back Franco Harris, and a tough defense. The game attracted a crowd of 52,878 to Three Rivers Stadium. It was San Francisco weather—partly sunny and 60 degrees.

In the first period, San Francisco barely had a chance on offense. They had the ball twice and failed to threaten either time. The Steelers got close once, but Harris fumbled on a first down play on the San Francisco 21 yard line. The period ended scoreless.

The first two times the 49ers had the ball in the second period they failed to get into Steeler territory. They made it the third time, thanks to the defense, as Wright picked off a Bradshaw pass and the 49ers took over on the Pittsburgh 46. Then Montana finally got the offense moving. In eight plays he steered the Niners toward the goal line, and completed a five-yard pass to Young for the touchdown. Wersching's conversion made it 7-0.

With only 26 seconds left in the half, the

49ers' defense produced another turnover. Playing before his hometown fans, Carlton Williamson recovered a Steeler fumble on the Pittsburgh 37 yard line. Two plays gained nine yards, which was enough for Wersching to kick a 45-yard field goal to give the 49ers a 10-0 halftime lead.

San Francisco took the second half kickoff and had a modest drive going. They had reached their own 42 yard line when cornerback Roy Blount intercepted Montana's pass at midfield and ran all the way for a touchdown. David Trout's conversion brought the Steelers within a field goal of tying at 10-7.

The next time the Niners had the ball they were again victimized by a Montana interception. Middle linebacker Jack Lambert picked it off to provide Pittsburgh with excellent field position on the San Francisco 22 yard line. Bradshaw immediately cashed in. He fired a 22-yard touchdown pass to Smith that put the Steelers in front for the first time, 14-10. San Francisco had a chance to come within a point of the Steelers near the end of the quarter, but Wersching's 37-yard field goal attempt was blocked.

The 49ers couldn't do anything the first time they got the ball in the fourth period. However, an interception by Williamson gave them another chance. Beginning on the Pittsburgh 43 yard line, Montana, who also was playing before hometown fans, led the 49ers to a touchdown in nine plays, with Walt Easley going around end for the final yard. Wersching's extra point sent the 49ers in front, 17-14.

The Niners still had to turn back one last threat by Pittsburgh. Starting from their own 17 yard line, the Steelers got to the San Francisco 36 before they were stopped. The 49ers had won another big game.

"This was our biggest physical test," Walsh said afterward. "Few teams come in here and win. That's why I'm so pleased with this young team. Our young defensive backs could be the best in football. It's just that simple."

San Francisco	0	10	0	7	17
Pittsburgh	0	0	14	0	14

San Francisco: 14:28, second period—Young 5-yard pass from Montana (Wersching, kick)

San Francisco: 14:57, second period—Wersching 45-yard field goal
Pittsburgh: 4:24, third period—Blount 50-yard interception return (Trout, kick)
Pittsburgh: 8:21, third period—Smith 22-yard pass from Bradshaw (Trout, kick)
San Francisco: 9:25, fourth period, Easley 1-yard run (Wersching, kick)

GAME TEN: ATLANTA

With a 7-2 record, the 49ers had exceeded even Walsh's expectations. They were riding the crest of a six game winning streak and at the same time enjoying a two game lead over both Los Angeles and Atlanta.

The setting couldn't have been better. The Falcons, who had convincingly beaten the 49ers the third week of the season, 34-17, arrived in San Francisco to meet the Niners for the second time. Atlanta couldn't afford to lose, since a defeat would leave them three games behind with only six games left in the regular schedule. A crowd of 59,127 came to see if the 49ers could, for all practical purposes, eliminate the Falcons from the Western Division race.

A closely played first quarter resulted in a scoreless board. The Falcons had failed to get a first down until the closing seconds, when they were awarded one on a penalty. And San Francisco's only serious thrust had been repelled when cornerback Kenny Johnson intercepted Montana's pass on the Atlanta 11 yard line.

But in the second quarter the game materialized into a fierce defensive struggle. Finally, with just 4:08 remaining, the Niners exploded from their 28 yard line in just two plays. The first was a 44-yard pass completion from Montana to Clark. A roughing-the-passer penalty on the play added 14 more yards. Then with the ball on the Atlanta 14 yard line, Montana looked for Solomon and completed a touchdown pass that sent the 49ers into the lead, 7-0. Less than a minute from the end of the first half, the 49ers got on the board again after Hicks intercepted Steve Bartkowski's pass on the San Francisco 45. Only nine seconds remained when Montana completed a 24-yard pass to Solomon on the Atlanta 31 yard line. Wersching came in and booted a 48-yard field goal as time ran out to

Bobby Leopold has one thing on his mind . . . Atlanta quarterback Steve Bartkowski.

With Montana holding, Ray Wersching kicks one of his four field goals against Cleveland.

give the 49ers a 10-0 halftime lead.

The Falcons finally solved the 49er defense in the third period. Bartkowski took them on a 75-yard drive in 16 plays, on a series that took 8:30. Then William Andrews scored the touchdown from a yard out to bring the Falcons close at 10-7. It was all the scoring anyone could produce as the period ended.

Montana answered back in the fourth period. He showed the Falcons how capable he was at grinding out an exhaustive drive. He led the 49ers on a 77-yard, 13-play effort that took 8:19. Montana also produced the touchdown with a three-yard pass to Young in the end zone. Wersching's conversion gave the Niners a 17-7 lead as 7:29 flashed on the scoreboard.

Atlanta struck with a scant 2:23 left in the

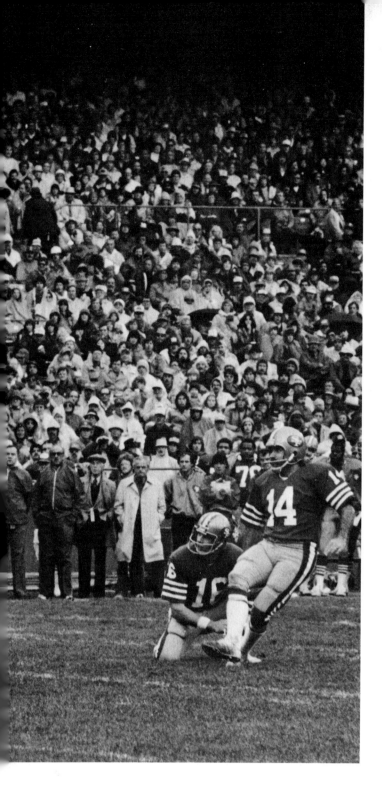

the ball on the San Francisco 42 yard line. Again, Bartkowski went to his passing game. His first throw was incomplete. However, he pressured the 49ers when he completed a 25-yard pass to Jenkins on the 17. He tried once more, but this time Hicks was ready. He intercepted Bartkowski's pass on the three yard line to reverse the Falcons and take the game.

"It's a great feeling to have a three game lead at this point in the season," said tight end Charle Young. "Right now we're just shooting for the playoffs but it's still one step at a time. The team has jelled as a unit. The addition of Dean and 'Hacksaw' and the development of our secondary has brought our defense around."

Atlanta	0	0	7	7	14
San Francisco	0	10	0	7	17

San Francisco: 11:08, second period—Solomon 14-yard pass from Montana (Wersching, kick)
San Francisco: 15:00, second period—Wersching 48-yard field goal
Atlanta: 10:40, third period, Andrews 1-yard run (Luckhurst, kick)
San Francisco: 7:41, fourth period—Young 3-yard pass from Montana (Wersching, kick)
Atlanta: 13:17, fourth period—Jackson 25-yard pass from Bartkowski (Luckhurst, kick)

GAME ELEVEN: CLEVELAND

The seven back-to-back victories were the most ever recorded by the 49ers in their NFL history, which goes back to 1950. The win over Atlanta also marked the second time in eleven years that the Niners had defeated all three Western Division opponents. The only other time was in 1974.

So much for history. San Francisco was riding high on top of the division with an 8-2 record. They had a three game advantage over both Atlanta and Los Angeles. If they could continue at their present performance level they would be hard to catch in the final six weeks of what was developing into the most exciting season in the club's history.

For the first time during the campaign, the 49ers had successive home games. The Cleveland Browns arrived in San Francisco for an inter-division meeting. They were having a disappointing season with a 4-6 record, but were considered dangerous because of quar-

tense struggle. Bartkowski moved quickly with his aerial attack. Starting in his own 24 yard line, he passed on every down. He threw six passes and completed five of them, the last one a 25-yard touchdown pass to Alfred Jenkins that sliced San Francisco's lead to 17-14 with only 1:43 left to play.

The Falcons weren't finished. They successfully executed an onside kick and recovered

terback Brian Sipe and some equally talented receivers.

Five minutes into the game, the 49ers missed an opportunity to score the first points when Wersching slipped on a field goal attempt. Montana had led a drive that started on the Niner 33 yard line and reached the Cleveland 23. And when Wersching tried a 40-yard field goal, he lost his footing and came up short.

The next time San Francisco had the ball, they suffered another misplay. Attempting to pass from his end zone, Montana was under a heavy rush. He made the mistake of throwing the ball away intentionally and was called for a safety, which gave the Browns a 2-0 lead. The period ended there.

Early in the second period the 49ers continued a drive that had started on their own 20 yard line. When they stalled on the Cleveland 10, Wersching kicked a 28-yard field goal that gave them a 3-2 lead. Then midway through the quarter, the Browns answered back as Matt Bahr booted a 28-yard field goal that restored Cleveland's lead, 5-3.

Wersching wasn't through. With only 1:07 left in the half, he put the finishing touches on a 50-yard drive by booting a 29-yard field goal. The low-scoring first half ended with San Francisco holding a slim 6-5 lead—more like a baseball score.

Six points were scored during third period action, on two field goals by Wersching. His first was a 28 yarder, midway through the quarter, and his second was for 29 yards, just one minute from the conclusion of the quarter, giving the 49ers a 12-5 boost.

The crowd, 52,445 strong, was restless as the fourth quarter began. Halfway through they grew concerned, as Sipe accounted for the game's first touchdown when he threw a 21-yard pass to wide receiver Reggie Rucker, and Bahr's conversion tied the game at 12-12.

Cleveland got the ball again with only 4:08 left. Starting on his own 34 yard line, Sipe directed the Browns all the way down to the San Francisco seven. Only 46 seconds were left as Bahr came in to kick a game-winning 24-yard field goal, giving Cleveland a 15-12 triumph. The 49ers' winning streak was snapped at seven.

"We're not terribly dejected," said Walsh. "Our failure to score touchdowns cost us the game. You can't be down there five times and come out with only 12 points. When a single touchdown beats you, you obviously have to improve."

Cleveland	2	3	0	10	15
San Francisco	0	6	6	0	12

Cleveland: 6:25, first period—Montana intentional grounding in end zone—safety
San Francisco: 3:32, second period—Wersching 28-yard field goal
Cleveland: 7:48, second period—Bahr 28-yard field goal
San Francisco: 13:53, second period—Wersching 29-yard field goal
San Francisco: 6:36, third period—Wersching 28-yard field goal
San Francisco: 14:00, third period—Wersching 28-yard field goal
Cleveland: 8:14, fourth period—Rucker 21-yard pass from Sipe (Bahr, kick)
Cleveland: 14:17, fourth period—Bahr 24-yard field goal

GAME TWELVE: LOS ANGELES

San Francisco's pride was bruised, but the loss to Cleveland did not get in the way of their quest for the Western Division championship. While they were upset by the Browns, the 49ers found some joy in learning that Los Angeles and Atlanta had also lost. With an 8-3 record, the 49ers were still three games in front of their two adversaries, both of whom had slipped to 5-6.

San Francisco was in an excellent position to eliminate the Rams in the season's 12th week of play, as they went to Anaheim to face the Rams for the second time. A win over Los Angeles would mark the first time since 1965 that the 49ers had been successful in beating the Rams twice in a single season. The game had personal significance for 'Hacksaw' Reynolds, who would be returning to Anaheim for the first time since he'd left the Rams after playing there for 11 years. What's more, they would be playing on his birthday.

Wersching got the 49ers on the scoreboard first by finishing a 62-yard, 11-play drive with a 47-yard field goal, to give the Niners a 3-0 lead. Those were the only points scored at the period's conclusion.

His counterpart, Frank Corral, got the Rams on the board in the opening minutes of the second quarter, booting a 44-yard field goal to tie the game at 3-3. The next time the Rams had the ball, they scored. Dan Pastorini directed an 80-yard drive in 11 plays, and capped it with a touchdown on a 22-yard pass to Wendell Tyler, giving Los Angeles a 10-3 lead. San Francisco came right back. Montana took them 74 yards on only five plays, with Davis cracking over from the one yard line to tie the game, 10-10.

However, the Rams put together another 80-yard march, this time in 13 plays. They scored just before the half ended when Mike Guman, on a pass-run option, threw a seven-yard completion to Preston Dennard to provide the Rams with a 17-10 halftime lead.

Amos Lawrence brought the crowd of 63,456 to its feet as the second half began when he took Corral's kickoff on the eight yard line and scampered 92 yards for a touchdown that tied the game a third time, 17-17. The play stunned the Rams and inspired the 49ers, who continued to score. First, Wersching broke the deadlock with a 34-yard field goal. Then Lott picked off Pastorini's pass and ran it back 26 yards for a touchdown that catapulted the Niners into a 27-17 advantage. Pat Haden took over for Pastorini and directed the Rams on their third 80-yard drive in nine plays. Then, just before the third period ended, he tossed a two-yard pass to tight end Walt Arnold to cut San Francisco's margin to 27-24.

Wersching entered the picture again some five minutes after the final period began. This time he kicked a 32-yard field goal that gave the Niners a 30-24 lead. Then the Rams took over. In a ball-controlled drive, Haden took them 90 yards in 15 plays, and Tyler smashed over from the one yard line to tie the game. Corral added the extra point to send the Rams in front, 31-30, with less than two minutes left to play.

Then Montana executed the two-minute offense. He got the Niners down to the Los Angeles 30 yard line, then, frantically trying to get the referee's attention, he called for time out. It was up to Wersching. His fourth field goal attempt would be his most important. With no time showing on the clock, Wersching booted a clutch 37-yard field goal that gave

the 49ers a 33-31 triumph. The Rams' season was over.

"This field goal rates right up there with the biggest of my career," Wersching exclaimed. "I've had a lot of game-winning kicks, but this was easily the biggest because I grew up here."

Walsh went beyond that.

"He's the greatest kicker in the history of the 49ers and perhaps the greatest in the game."

San Francisco	3	7	17	6	33
Los Angeles	0	17	7	7	31

San Francisco: 7:27, first period—Wersching 47-yard field goal
Los Angeles: 1:03, second period—Corral 44-yard field goal
Los Angeles: 9:00, second period—Tyler 22-yard pass from Pastorini (Corral, kick)
San Francisco: 11:13, second period—Davis 1-yard run (Wersching, kick)
Los Angeles: 14:37, second period—Dennard 7-yard pass from Guman (Corral, kick)
San Francisco: 0:18, third period—Lawrence 92-yard kickoff return (Wersching, kick)
San Francisco: 6:36, third period—Wersching 34-yard field goal
San Francisco: 9:27, third period—Lott 26-yard interception return (Wersching, kick)
Los Angeles: 12:56, third period—Arnold 2-yard pass from Haden (Corral, kick)
San Francisco: 4:50, fourth period—Wershing 32-yard field goal
Los Angeles: 13:09, fourth period — Tyler 1-yard run (Corral, kick)
San Francisco: 15:00, fourth period—Wersching 37-yard field goal.

GAME THIRTEEN: NEW YORK GIANTS

It was there for the taking. The 49ers needed only one more victory to clinch their first Western Division championship in nine years.

Surprisingly, at the game against the New York Giants there were 3,895 no-shows at Candlestick Park. A crowd of 57,186 turned out on the cool, clear afternoon to see if the 49ers could make it official. Although Atlanta was still a contender, it would take a total 49er collapse to keep them from the crown.

The game would also be a big one for the Giants, despite the fact that they had a 6-6 record. Hoping for a shot at a wild card berth

Dan Bunz nails Giant running back Rob Carpenter just as he gets past the line of scrimmag

Mike Wilson manages to get a step on Cincinnati safety Ken Riley.

in the playoffs, every game now was crucial.

San Francisco had the first chance to score and blew it. Montana had led the offense on the field and they got as far as the Giants' 19 yard line, but when Wersching came on to attempt a 36-yard field goal, it was blocked.

The next time they made it work. The offense was provided with an excellent opportunity when Hicks intercepted quarterback Scott Brunner's pass on the San Francisco 30 yard line and brought it back 54 yards to the New York 16. Seven plays later, Davis plunged over from the one yard line and San Francisco moved into a 7-0 lead, which didn't change when the period ended five minutes later.

Once more, the defense created a turnover that allowed the 49ers to score again. On the first play of the second quarter Rob Carpenter fumbled a pitchout and Keena Turner recovered it on the New York 40 yard line. It only took the 49ers five plays to score. On a well-executed third and three play, Montana went up the middle on a quarterback draw for a 20-yard touchdown run. Wershing's conversion made it 14-0.

Some ten minutes later, Wersching tried

another field goal, this time from the 40 yard line. However, he slipped slightly as he approached the ball and his kick hit the right upright. With 1:29 left on the clock, Joe Danelo boomed a 52-yard field goal that put the Giants onto the board at intermission, 14-3.

That score remained throughout the entire third quarter. San Francisco only had the ball twice, and failed to threaten either time. And as the period drew to a close, the Giants were working on a long drive that brought them to the San Francisco three yard line.

On the first play of the fourth quarter the Giants scored. Carpenter bounced off the line and into the end zone to complete a 76-yard drive in 11 plays. Danelo's kick reduced the 49ers' margin to 14-10, with practically a whole period left to play.

Montana then masterminded a drive that took up half of the remaining time. Beginning on his own 22 yard line, he took the Niners all the way down to the New York one yard line, only to miss a touchdown when Ring was stopped on third down from a yard out. But Wersching kicked a 23-yard field goal that stretched the 49er margin to 17-10. The drive had covered 72 yards in 16 plays and consumed 7:27.

From then on, it was up to the defense, and they held the Giants for the rest of the game. When the action was over, the 49ers were the champions of the West. It was the sixth game that San Francisco had won by seven or less points, but it was by far the biggest.

"I think everybody realizes how far we can go." said Keith Fahnhorst in the happy 49er locker room. "It feels good to have it wrapped up, but none of us will be satisfied with just the Western Division championship."

New York	0	3	0	7	10
San Francisco	7	7	0	3	17

San Francisco: 10:13, first period—Davis 1-yard run (Wersching, kick)
San Francisco: 2:56, second period—Montana 20-yard run (Wersching, kick)
New York: 13:36, second period—Danelo 52-yard field goal
New York: 0:06, fourth period—Carpenter 3-yard run (Danelo, kick)
San Francisco: 7:43, fourth period—Wersching 23-yard field goal

GAME FOURTEEN: CINCINNATI

There was no way under the sun that San Francisco could wind up flat against the Cincinnati Bengals in Cincinnati, a week after their championship celebration. Walsh wouldn't allow it. Or rather, his players wouldn't allow it.

They knew how much the game meant to Walsh personally. It was at Cincinnati that Walsh had coached for eight years (and had coached Cincinnati quarterback Ken Anderson personally), with the hope of becoming the Bengals' head coach when Paul Brown retired. When he wasn't chosen it was the first in a series of disappointments for Walsh, and now he was returning to Cincinnati for the first time since he'd taken over the 49ers three years ago.

Cincinnati was also playoff bound. They had the same record as the 49ers, 10-3, and, with the exception of Dallas, was the only team to win as many games. A crowd of 56,796 turned out for a possible playoff preview.

Montana reassured Walsh almost at once. He took over after Cincinnati was stopped following the kickoff, and led the 49ers on a 66-yard drive that encompassed 15 plays and consumed 7:59. The touchdown was a short four-yard pass to Bill Ring. Montana had been brilliant. He'd completed five of eight passes. And more important, three of these completions had come on third down plays.

Then the Bengals threatened, but Keena Turner stopped them by intercepting Anderson's pass on the 10 yard line. The quarter ended soon after with San Francisco still in front, 7-0. Jim Breech succeeded in booting a 30-yard field goal 2:28 before the half to trim the 49ers' margin to 7-3, concluding a 61-yard drive in 11 plays. When Breech's kickoff sailed into the end zone, giving San Francisco the ball on the 20 yard line, it looked as though the Niners would run out the clock.

Montana fooled everyone and came out throwing. He threw eight times out of the ten plays he called and carried the 49ers to a touchdown. The payoff was a 15-yard strike to Clark with just eight seconds showing on the clock. Wersching added the conversion that gave the Niners a 14-3 halftime edge.

The defenses of both teams played hard through a scoreless third period, when neither the 49ers nor the Bengals seriously threatened to score. Intensity and hard-hitting were evident on both sides.

In the fourth period it was San Francisco's defense that set up the final scoring when Hicks recovered a Bengal fumble on the Cincinnati 40 yard line. Montana took it from there. Eight plays later, he scored from a yard out to seal the victory with 6:27 remaining in the game. Wersching added the conversion to give the 49ers a sweet 21-3 triumph—their eleventh of the season.

Although the statistics were about even, the San Francisco defense had made the difference. They'd intercepted three passes and recovered the same number of fumbles, while forcing Anderson from the game with an injury early in the third period.

"We didn't spend a lot of time talking about Cincinnati," said Walsh, "but we really didn't have to. We talked about maintaining our hard-hitting standard of play. Our players made a pact that they would continue to hit just as hard as always. I feel terrific. It was a fantastic experience to come back and do this well."

Ronnie Lott concurred. "We felt Cincinnati really hadn't been hit since New Orleans. We had hoped to hit hard and get a few turnovers."

| San Francisco | | | | | 7 | 7 | 0 | 7 | 21 |
| Cincinnati | | | | | 0 | 3 | 0 | 0 | 3 |

San Francisco: 7:59, first period—Ring 4-yard pass from Montana (Wersching, kick)
Cincinnati: 12:28, second period—Breech 30-yard field goal
San Francisco: 14:58, second period—Clark 15-yard pass from Montana (Wersching, kick)
San Francisco: 8:32, fourth period—Montana 1-yard run (Wersching, kick)

GAME FIFTEEN: HOUSTON

San Francisco had proven itself the hottest team in football. The 49ers were on a roll, having won 10 of their last 11 games to balloon their record to 11-3. Only the Dallas Cowboys, whom the Niners had trounced earlier in the season, could match the best record in the NFL.

The 49ers had no intention of stopping now. Their objective in the final two weeks of the season was to gain the home team advantage in the playoffs, and they had to outperform Dallas to do so.

Their first obstacle was the Houston Oilers, who were the 49ers' final regular season home opponent. The Oilers were finishing a disappointing campaign with a 6-8 record and experiencing a major change at quarterback. Gifford Nielsen had taken over for Ken Stabler, who had been an Oakland favorite a couple of years ago.

A light rain kept the crowd down to 55,707. It looked as though the 49ers would score the first time they got the ball. With Montana calling the signals, they drove from their 12 yard line to Houston's two yard line. But they couldn't punch the ball across for a touchdown. Davis was stopped for no-gain on fourth down when he tried to go over from the one yard line. Neither team mounted a threat after that and the quarter ended with no score.

The action in the second period resembled that in the opening quarter. Each team crossed midfield only once. Neither team came close to getting any points, and the contest remained scoreless at the halfway point.

Apparently the halftime respite was what was needed by the 49ers. They took the kickoff and went 69 yards in 10 plays for the game's first touchdown. Ricky Patton scored from three yards out and Wersching added the conversion to give the Niners a 7-0 lead.

They extended it to 14-0 the next time they got the ball following a Houston punt. This time they marched 65 yards in nine plays, with Earl Cooper getting the touchdown in a three-yard sweep around left end. The third time San Francisco acquired possession they scored again, only they didn't have to go so far. Craig Puki had recovered a Houston fumble on the Oiler 26 yard line to set the stage, and four plays later Montana rolled to his left and hit Clark with a two-yard touchdown pass that extended the Niners' bulge to 21-0. When the period ended, San Francisco was in command, and Guy Benjamin replaced Montana.

He picked up where Montana left off. After

Earl Cooper jumps with joy after scoring a touchdown against Houston

running two plays at the end of the third period, Benjamin continued to move the 49ers in the fourth period. The result was that he completed a 76-yard drive in 10 plays, finishing it with a five-yard scoring pass to Mike Wilson as the 49ers stretched their lead to 28-0.

The only remaining question was whether the 49ers defense would register a shutout. It didn't happen. Houston went 59 yards in eight plays on their final drive, helped along by two pass interference penalties. Earl Campbell then scored Houston's only touchdown from the one-yard line with just 47 seconds left in the game. Toni Fritsch's extra point try was blocked by Dwaine Board and the 49ers had their 12th win, 28-6. The victory tied the all-time club record that had been established in the old All-American Conference in 1948.

It was also a big game for Cooper. He finished with 115 yards rushing and receiving, his highest total of the season. Cooper had also scored his first touchdown of the year in the third quarter, and was given a game ball for his performance.

"We wanted to use this game as a learning experience," said Walsh, " and in some ways it was. Our back-up players showed well, especially Guy Benjamin, and that has to help us later on."

Houston	0	0	0	6	6
San Francisco	0	0	21	7	28

San Francisco: 6:04, third period—Patton 3-yard run (Wersching, kick)
San Francisco: 11:13, third period—Cooper 3-yard run (Wersching, kick)
San Francisco: 13:26, third period—Clark 2-yard pass from Montana (Wersching, kick)
San Francisco: 5:45, fourth period—Wilson 27-yard pass from Benjamin (Wersching, kick)
Houston: 14:13, fourth period—Campbell 1-yard run

GAME SIXTEEN: NEW ORLEANS

One game remained. With San Francisco assured of a spot in the playoffs, it would be a game in which the 49ers had to convince themselves of winning even though they had earned the home field advantage the day before, when Dallas was surprised by the New York Giants in overtime, 13-10. That left San Francisco with the best record on the NFL, but they had to win to maintain it.

The 49ers' final regular season game was in New Orleans. Earlier in the year, they had defeated the Saints, 21-14, for their second victory of the campaign and one that launched them on an eight-game winning streak. In that game, quarterback Archie Manning had been hampered by an injury and didn't play until the final period. Now he was back in top form. So was rookie running back George Rogers, who was in pursuit of the NFL rushing title, and needed a big game in achieving it.

When the Saints couldn't advance following the opening kickoff, the 49ers struck. Montana sparked a 72-yard drive with his passing to get the Niners a touchdown in 10 plays. The touchdown pass was a 13-yarder to Charle Young. Wersching converted and the 49ers jumped into a 7-0 lead.

Then for some reason, San Francisco couldn't hang on to the ball. A couple of costly fumbles allowed the Saints to take over the lead. The first was when Freddie Solomon fumbled a punt and New Orleans recovered on the San Francisco 18 yard line. Rogers carried four straight times and finally scored from the one yard line. Benny Ricardo's extra point tied the game at 7-7.

The second 49er mistake occurred on the ensuing kickoff. Amos Lawrence fumbled the ball, picked it up and then fumbled it again. New Orleans recovered on the seven yard line. After Jack Holmes got to the five, Rogers took over. He was stopped for no-gain on his first carry but then swept around right end to score the Saints' second touchdown in less than two minutes. Ricardo added the conversion to give New Orleans a 14-7 edge as the period came to a close.

Montana moved the 49ers as the second quarter began, leading them on a 69-yard drive that required nine plays and 4:07. He got the touchdown on a two-yard pass to Solomon, who got loose in the end zone. Wersching added the conversion to tie the game at 14-14.

When the Niners got the ball again, Guy Benjamin replaced Montana. This had a special significance for Benjamin who had been with the Saints before he was acquired by the 49ers. And he almost sparked the 49ers to a

Montana tries to stay in bounds as Charle Young takes care of two Saint defenders.

touchdown. Beginning on the San Francisco 33 yard line, he took advantage of his ground game to get the 49ers to the New Orleans five yard line. However, his third down pass intended for Clark was intercepted in the end zone, and the half ended with the teams deadlocked at 14-14.

Late in the third period the Saints broke the tie. New Orleans got good field position by bottling up the 49ers on their three yard line. Starting on the Niners' 36 following Jim Miller's punt, Manning got them to the 10 yard line before Ricardo booted a 27-yard field goal that sent New Orleans in front, 17-14. The quarter ended two minutes later.

San Francisco bounced back in the fourth period. Mixing his plays well, Benjamin drove the 49ers 79 yards in just seven plays, hitting on all three passes he threw. Davis ran for the touchdown from three yards out to put the 49ers back on top. Then Wersching added the

point to give them a 21-17 lead. New Orleans had one more chance and failed, and the 49ers finished with the best record in the NFL, 13-3, by winning their fifth straight game.

"Regardless of what happens in the playoffs, at least I'll be able to sit back and take pride in what I feel to be indicative of the effort that this team has displayed throughout the entire season," said Walsh.

San Francisco	7	7	0	7	21
New Orleans	14	0	3	0	17

San Francisco: 6:33, first period—Young 13-yard pass from Montana (Wersching, kick)
New Orleans: 13:01, first period—Rogers 6-yard run (Ricardo, kick)
New Orleans: 14:47, first period—Rogers 5-yard run (Ricardo, kick)
San Francisco: 3:54, second period—Solomon 2-yard pass from Montana (Wersching, kick)
New Orleans: 12:25, third period—Ricardo 27-yard field goal
San Francisco: 7:47, fourth period—Davis 3-yard run (Wersching, kick)

133

GIANTS PLAYOFF

The rain was incessant. By the end of the week, the Bay area was plagued with floods and mud slides. No one could remember the last time rain had so severely drenched the city, and the January sky gave no hope for relief. The most optimistic weather forecast was that the rain would stop on game day, just as the 49ers and the New York Giants took to the field.

Meanwhile, the field at the team's training compound in Redwood City was a quagmire. Walsh had had to arrange for practices indoors at a local high school, then later at Stanford University. Now that they knew the wild card winner in the contest between the Giants and the Philadelphia Eagles, practice time was vital. Walsh was making the best of a bad situation. But he had gotten his team too far to let rain or anything else block the road to the Super Bowl.

"We've had two inches of rain in the last 24 hours," he said at the time. "That's very unseasonal. It looks like there'll be more of it today. At this point, I don't know if the Giants will be able to practice at Candlestick Park on Saturday as they've planned. It's up to the city officials. I'm hoping they don't. I hope they save the field for both of us on Sunday."

No one would venture to say what the playing surface at Candlestick would be like. A tarpaulin had been spread over the field to help protect it. Unless the Giants used the field, it wouldn't be removed until early Sunday morning. But since the drainage at the stadium wasn't considered adequate, no one knew what the field would be like.

"Once they remove the tarp it's hard to say what will be under there," Walsh said. "A lot of fishing worms, I guess."

Walsh and his counterpart, Ray Perkins of the Giants, weren't the only ones concerned about the playing conditions for such an important game. The officials of the National Football League in New York were also worried. After dozens of phone calls to San Francisco, the powers at the league office decided to dispatch George Toma to survey the situation.

Toma may not be a household name to pro football fans around the country, but he is held in high esteem in the boardroom of every NFL club. Short and good-natured, Toma is the chief groundskeeper for Kansas City's dual stadium complex. Someday there may be a special mention of him in the pro football Hall of Fame in Canton, Ohio. The reason: he has been involved in more Super Bowls than any player and he has made many major contributions to the game. Every year since 1967 the NFL has commissioned him to appear at the Super Bowl site a week before the event, to insure ideal playing conditions. Several years ago, in Super Bowl XIV, when five days of heavy rains had transformed its field into a shallow lake, Toma performed his magic and prevented Pasadena's famed Rose Bowl from turning into a mud bowl.

Now this would be the second time in a month that Toma had been sent to San Francisco's Candlestick Park. Back in December, when the 49ers had clinched a home field advantage in the championship playoffs, the league sent him out to work on the soft, muddy terrain. Candlestick Park's poor drainage facilities had left the ground so wet that just walking on it lifted clumps of sod loose. After a few days Toma had the field in excellent shape—until the torrential rains a few weeks later.

Many fans felt that the muddy field would benefit the Giants. Down through the years, it's been determined that a slow field was more advantageous to a running game than a passing game, and passing was the strength of the San Francisco offense. Perkins concurred with that reasoning, and was brimming with confidence.

"In the history of the game, if you check into it, a muddy field favors the team that can run the ball the best," he said as the Giants got ready.

It's obvious that Perkins had Rob Carpenter in mind when he referred to the Giants' running game. The Giants would probably not have advanced in the playoffs without the efforts of the squat, powerful running back. Carpenter had carried the ball 33 times and had run for a career high of 161 yards against the Eagles—reason enough for Walsh to single him out as the best running back in the playoffs. He was well aware of what Carpenter meant to the Giants' offense.

Since Carpenter joined the Giants from Houston after the fourth game of the season, the Giants were 8-5. Two of the defeats occurred when Carpenter was injured and didn't play. He ran over 100 yards in each of

five games, and significantly, the Giants won all of those games. Furthermore, because of Carpenter's efforts, Perkins was able to utilize a ball-control, conservative attack that, in essence, helped screen the inexperience of quarterback Scott Brunner, and allowed the Giants' defense, ranked second in the NFC, to dominate the action. Carpenter, who was thought of as Earl Campbell's blocker during his last three years in Houston, was now the key to the Giants' ground game. He had performed consistently, despite running behind a makeshift line the last month of the season.

"We are just now starting to get a feel for one another," Carpenter said as the San Francisco game drew near. "I like to run where I read blocks, and go in one direction while they block their man in another. It takes time to learn how each guy does his job. That's why the Eagles game meant so much for me. When I was with Houston, what I did there might have meant a first down or keeping a drive alive. But what I did against the Eagles affected the outcome of the game. For the first time, I had a major role in determining a playoff game. That's a big change, and that's why that game was the greatest football day of my life."

Carpenter and the Giants were no strangers to the 49ers. They had faced each other during the regular season, on November 29, in a game that was significant for San Francisco. Not only did the 49ers defeat the Giants, 17-10, but in doing so they clinched the Western Division title. On that day the 49ers extended their record to 10-3 and became the first team in any division of the NFL to clinch a playoff berth. With that game the Giants' record slipped to 6-7, and nobody gave them much chance of making the playoffs.

In that game the Giants' star runner only managed 40 yards on 13 carries, although he did score the team's only touchdown early in the final quarter. Quarterback Scott Brunner only connected on 13 of 34 passes, for 162 yards. Three of his passes were intercepted.

Even so, the Giants appeared confident this time, emphasizing that the 49ers really hadn't beaten them in the first game—the Giants had beaten themselves. Their receivers had dropped eight of Brunner's passes, and there

Craig Puki (54) and Jack Reynolds (64) combine to stop a Giant receiver.

Jack Reynolds fights off a block.

had been three interceptions, three sacks, two lost fumbles and four holding penalties. As Perkins put it, "we were self-destructing. They made the plays and we didn't." And, although the offense had been ineffective, the fact was that the defense *had* performed well.

Now, with the playoff game before him, Perkins knew he needed more offense. He was especially concerned with first down plays. It would be crucial for his team to produce sizeable yardage on first down in order to keep Fred Dean, the 49ers' excellent pass rusher, on the sidelines. Neutralizing Dean would give the Giants' offense more options in their ball-control attack. The primary goal on defense would be to stop Joe Montana on first down, and to disrupt San Francisco's own ball-control tendencies—which rely to a large ex-

tent on the short pass. This would allow the Giants' superb rookie linebacker, Lawrence Taylor, more opportunities to blitz from his weakside position.

"Dean puts a lot of pressure on you," said Brunner. "If we can get four or five yards on first down, it will keep the third down distances shorter."

Actually, the first time the teams met, the 49er offense hadn't exactly been overpowering. They'd had possession of the ball 13 times, but ten of those possessions had begun in their own territory. Only three times had they generated enough offense to cross midfield—resulting in a single field goal. The two touchdowns they scored occurred when they began drives in New York's end of the field. On the whole, San Francisco's offense was a bit on the conservative side. Sixteen of quarterback Joe Montana's completions were to running backs. They scored first and let the defense do the rest.

"I think we wanted to play just soundly enough to come out with the victory," Montana explained. "We didn't want to make those big mistakes and give the ballgame to them. Now we've seen how good they've gotten over the past few weeks. They've beaten some good teams. Their offense, especially, has improved. We can't be too conservative this time. We've still got to take chances downfield, and I think we'll do it."

Regardless of the condition of the field on Sunday, it was imperative that the 49ers take the Giants very seriously this time. For one thing, the Giants with their menacing defense had been among the hottest teams in the NFL for the final quarter of the season. Behind the tall, lanky Brunner, they had closed strongly, winning four of their last five regular season encounters. Their defense had squelched the high-scoring Dallas Cowboys in the final game of the year. When they handcuffed the Eagles the following week in the wild card playoff in Philadelphia, they actually entertained visions of making it all the way to the Super Bowl. Brunner was gaining experience with each game and the Giants had won five of the six games he started, which is what Super Bowl aspirations are made of.

"The first two or three times he started, he had a tendency to overthink," Perkins said. "He's always been a good classroom student, but there's only so much you can learn without playing. He's learning from experience now, and I think that was evident last week against the Eagles. Now he has become very confident and poised. He's been in pressure situations. He pulled out two games at the end. That's pressure football."

The fact remained that the Giants' strength throughout the season had been their defense. Although only a rookie, Taylor made a big difference. His speed and savvy enabled him to come up with the big play, game after game. He loved to blitz from his outside position. For running backs assigned to block him, his power was too much to contain. In all, he was a disruptive force that the 49ers had to eliminate.

Montana, the leading passer in the NFC, offered the ultimate challenge to Taylor and the rest of the Giant defense. Montana is patient, intelligent and unpredictably dangerous when driven from the pocket. He has good movement to his left or right when he rolls out, and he is not easy to contain even when being pressured. Perkins considered Montana the best quarterback the Giants had faced all year. The New York coach acknowledged that Montana was able to accept short yardage on ball-controlled passes. Perkins was willing to accept the strategy because the San Francisco ground attack is weak. It was Perkins' belief that if Montana threw enough passes, they would either result in incompletions, or better yet, interceptions—even sacks. That's how much confidence Perkins had in his defense.

"When you get up against the great defenses, you must execute or they take you apart," said Walsh. "We're proving you can throw the short pass and win. Against us, teams have been passing on first down a lot to keep Dean off the field; but if that first down pass is incomplete, here he comes! And because he won't play every down, if we're ahead in the fourth quarter, he'll be fresh.

"We are crossing our fingers about Candlestick. I haven't seen it since the last time we played on it. We assume that it is going to be very wet. The thing about the field is that it is deceiving. It is rather treacherous where it doesn't appear to be. And that is how players can sometimes be fooled by it. If you were an aerial circus like San Diego, the field could hurt. We can bore the fans to tears with our passing game. A field like this favors a conservative game. You are not going to get great footing. There are certain running plays you wouldn't attempt, certain passing plays you wouldn't attempt either.

"If you look at our films, we're slipping and falling, but then you see the other team doing it, too. It adds an element of chance to the game: a man can unexpectedly slip as he is covering a receiver or a receiver can slip running a pattern. Both can be disastrous. We beat them the first time, but it gives no psychological advantage. When you get to the playoffs, you start over. Now, it's another game."

Yet, it was more than that to loyal 49er fans. This was the first playoff game in San Francisco since 1972. Notwithstanding the week-long rain and the forecast, 60,994 tickets were sold. Overcast skies delivered a light rain just before kickoff, convincing 2,634 ticketholders to remain at home instead. Because of the dampness, it felt colder than the 45 degrees recorded, but the 58,360 diehards who showed up were unperturbed. The 49ers won the coin-toss and elected to receive the opening kickoff. The cheering began as Bill Ring braced himself for Joe Danelo's kick.

Ring had difficulty handling the kick. He managed, however, to recover the ball on the 15 yard line. Montana led the offense on-field. He didn't wait long to pass. On the very first play of the game, he located Dwight Clark for a 16-yard gain. Ricky Patton added five more on a quick trap up the middle. On second and five from the 36 yard line, Montana caught the Giants by surprise by throwing deep. But his long pass, intended for Freddie Solomon, was overthrown. Then he generated excitement on his third down play by completing a pass to Patton in the flat, who managed to break away from several tacklers and speed down the sidelines for an apparent touchdown. However, Solomon, anxious to spring Patton with a block, was called for clipping on the Giants' 36 yard line.

After the penalty, San Francisco began again from its own 49 yard line. Earl Cooper could only gain a yard, and Montana was sacked for a nine-yard loss on second down. They fell further back when a five-yard false start penalty left the ball on the 36. Facing a third and 23, Montana tried a pass to Patton that fell incomplete. The only alternative was to punt. Jim Miller did so, and his punt rolled dead on the New York 26. Then San Francisco got a break. The Giants were penalized five yards for defensive holding; but, more important, the penalty carried an automatic first down.

Montana went back to work on his 41 yard line. He called a pass and then proceeded to hit rookie Mike Wilson for a 15-yard gain. Again, Montana dropped back to pass. This time he threw an 11-yard completion to Clark

on the Giants' 33 yard line. The 49ers were moving now. For the third straight time, Montana decided to pass. This time, he sent Clark on a deeper pattern and hit him with a 22 yard aerial.

San Francisco had an excellent opportunity now to score first. They had a first down on the 11 yard line as they resumed their attack. Patton picked up two yards to the nine. Montana returned to the air. A holding penalty on Fred Quillan unexpectedly sent the 49ers back to the 18 yard line. Undaunted, Montana quickly hit Solomon on the right side for 11 yards to the eight. Looking around in the huddle, the 49ers' quarterback called Charle Young's number on a crucial third down play. It worked. Montana drilled an on-target eight-yard pass into the veteran tight end's hands for a touchdown. Wersching added the extra point to give San Francisco a 7-0 lead.

The Giants began conservatively when they put the ball in play on their own 23 yard line following the kickoff. Carpenter carried the ball three straight times for a total of 11 yards and a first down. Brunner then threw two high percentage passes—one to tight end Dave Young for five yards and the other to Carpenter for 10 yards and another Giant first down on the 49. Carpenter carried again for two yards to the San Francisco 49. On second down, the 49er defense forced a turnover. Hampered by the rush, Brunner dumped a short three-yard pass to Carpenter. Jack Reynolds jarred the ball loose and Bobby Leopold recovered the fumble on the San Francisco 46.

On first down the Niners were penalized 15 yards back to their 31 when Solomon was flagged a second time for clipping. Montana brought them right back with a 16-yard completion to Clark on the 47. After Patton got to midfield, Montana attempted a deep third down pass to Cooper that was incomplete. Miller was called on to punt again and the Giants returned on offense for the second time on their 28 yard line. Leon Perry tried the right side and was stopped for no gain by Dwaine Board. Then, Brunner stunned the 49ers. He found wide receiver Earnest Gray open over the middle and hit him on the run.

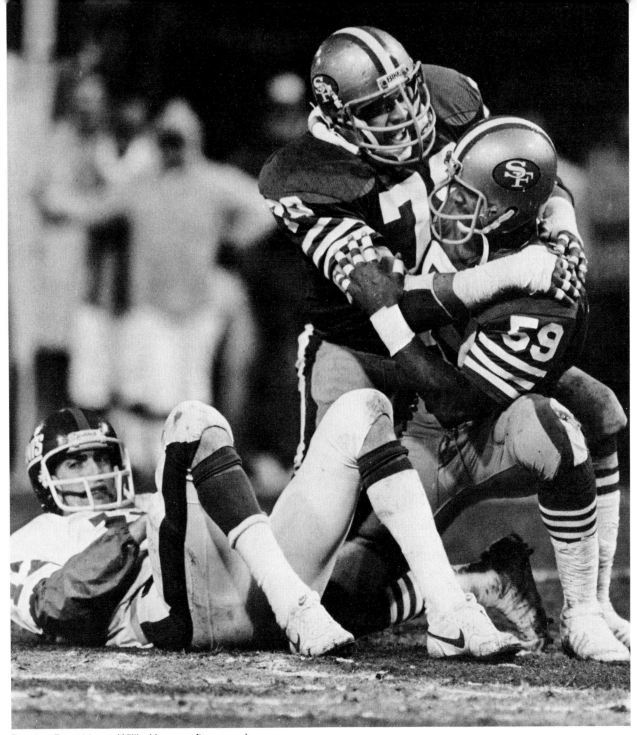

Dwaine Board hugs Willie Harper after a sack.

Without breaking stride, Gray ran untouched into the end zone for a touchdown. Danelo tied the game with his conversion. The speed and finesse of the big play sobered the 49ers.

A moment later, Amos Lawrence brought the crowd to its feet. He took the kickoff on the five yard line and almost broke it for a touchdown. Racing to his left, he was finally brought down on the New York 48. The dynamic return gave the Niners excellent field position. Montana passed and connected with Solomon for 11 yards to the 37. On the very next play, Patton started to run right but changed direction. In doing this, he fumbled but fortunately recovered the ball on the 44 for a seven-yard loss. It didn't bother Montana in the least. He dispatched Clark deep down the right sideline and found him all alone with a 39-yard pass on the New York five-yard line. The Niners were back looking for gold.

Montana tried to get it with a short pass to Cooper that was broken up in the end zone.

Ring was sent into the game and picked up two yards. On third down he was stopped for no gain on the three. The gun sounded to end the first period. Montana went over to the sidelines to confer with Walsh. The decision was to go for the field goal and thus take over the lead. When the second period began, Wersching booted a 22-yard field goal that broke the tie. San Francisco had a 10-7 advantage.

Following the kickoff, the Giants lined up on their 37 yard line. Brunner passed short to Carpenter for five yards. On second down, Brunner recovered his own fumble. Employing the shotgun formation, he tried to pass down the middle to his other wide receiver, Johnny Perkins. However, Dwight Hicks succeeded in tipping the ball away from Perkins and Ronnie Lott alertly intercepted on San Francisco's 35. He returned the ball to the Giant 38 only to have it brought back to the Niners' 32 yard line because of clipping.

Montana tried to connect with Solomon on first down but Mark Haynes knocked the pass away. Cooper then found some daylight and busted through for 10 yards and a first down on the 42. Montana detected something as the 49ers set up and called time out. After talking with Walsh, telling him that the Giants were over-playing the run, he returned to the huddle. He diagrammed a play to Solomon called Pass 90. The beautiful play-action fake to Patton momentarily froze the Giant defense. It enabled Solomon to slip behind the Giants' zone coverage and latch onto Montana's 58-yard touchdown pass. It was a stroke of genius. Wersching's conversion stretched the 49er margin to 17-7.

They didn't wait long to add to it. Leon Bright fumbled on the first play after the kickoff when he was jolted by Craig Puki. The loose ball was recovered by Keena Turner on the Giant 42. The 49er offense returned to the field to the cheers of the crowd, who sensed a blow-out if San Francisco could score another quick touchdown. Montana started the Niners on their way with a 14-yard pass completion to Young. A short pass to Solomon took them three yards to the 25. Montana then reverted to the run. He handed the ball to Patton who eluded inside linebacker Brian Kelly's tackle.

Willie Harper leaps high to in attempt to block a pass.

Patton got to the outside and ran down the right sidelines behind a finishing block by Dan Audick for a 25-yard touchdown gallop, the longest such run by the 49ers all season. Wersching kicked the extra point to send San Francisco flying, 24-7. San Francisco had scored 17 points in just 4:33.

Still, the Giants hung on. Starting on their own 19, they put a drive together. Carpenter got five yards then shook loose for 13 more. Getting only three yards on Carpenter's next carry, Brunner passed 16 yards to Gray for a first down on the San Francisco 49. Carpenter again got the call and gained five to the 44. After Brunner's second down pass fell incomplete, he lined up in a shotgun and tossed a 14-yard pass to Perkins for a first down on the 30. The Niner secondary stiffened. Brunner attempted three straight passes; all three were defended successfully. The Giants were forced to settle for a 48-yard field goal by Danelo that reduced San Francisco's margin, 24-10.

There were just over five minutes remaining when the Niners came out on offense from their 27. Patton managed a yard before Montana threw a 17-yard bullet to Solomon. Cooper got two yards and Montana came right back to Solomon with a seven-yard pass on the New York 46. On a third and one, Cooper exploded. Following the blocking of Patton and Ayers, the big fullback churned for 20 yards to the Giant 26 as the clock signalled the two-minute warning.

After the time-out, the Giant defense answered back. Defensive end George Martin put the squeeze on Montana, forcing him to throw away a pass. Nose tackle Bill Neill then nailed Montana for a two-yard loss on a quarterback draw. Finally, outside linebacker Brad Van Pelt sacked Montana for a four-yard loss back to the 32. As the first half neared an end, Wersching was asked to attempt a 50-yard field goal, but his kick was short and wide to the left.

The 49ers had maintained total control of the opening half. Montana was picking the Giant zone defense apart with his skillful execution of play-action passing. He completed 15 of 22 passes for 276 yards and two touchdowns, without being intercepted. The offense generated 325 total yards while the defense held Carpenter to 41 yards running and Brunner to 125 passing. It remained to be seen if the rain would bother the 49ers for the second half.

The Giants opened their attack in the same manner in which they began the game, namely by giving the ball to Carpenter. Beginning on the 11 yard line, Carpenter ran for five yards and then four. When he tried to gain a yard for a first down, Dan Bunz turned him back. Dave Jennings then punted, reaching the San Francisco 36 yard line without a return.

Patton found only three yards in the middle as Niner fans hoped for a game-clinching touchdown. Running well, Cooper streaked around left end for 14 yards before being brought down on the Giant 39. The 49ers appeared to be heading for paydirt. Then, without warning they were thwarted. Montana, of all people, made a sophomoric mistake that pumped new life into the Giants' wobbly game. He wanted to toss a short five-yard pass to Solomon. Feeling the rush of right end Gary Jeter and outside linebacker Bryon Hunt, Montana threw the ball up for grabs in the direction of Patton. Strong safety Bill Currier instantly swooped in and picked the ball off.

The Giants took over on their 41. Brunner went for the bomb on the very first play. He sent Perkins deep, and the fleet-footed receiver ran between Lott and safety Dwight Hicks, where Brunner delivered a perfect pass for a 59-yard touchdown. The Giants stunned the 49ers with their second big play touchdown pass. When Danelo converted to put the score at 24-17, New York was only a touchdown away. There was still 11:22 left to play in the third period.

Lawrence's 19-yard kickoff return gave the Niners decent field position on their 36. Montana began smartly with a 10-yard pass to Patton on the 46. On the next play, a holding penalty seemed to upset the 49ers. Their attack suddenly collapsed. First, Montana threw an incomplete pass. Then he was sacked by Taylor for a three-yard loss. On third down, a screen pass to Lenvil Elliott only produced five yards. Miller had to punt the Niners out of trouble.

San Francisco's defense held the Giants in

check following Miller's kick. After Carpenter got two yards to the 31, Brunner missed on a pass to Young. Trying for third down, the Giants employed the shotgun. On a crossing pattern down the middle, Brunner fired a 30-yard aerial to Gray, who almost broke away before being stopped on the San Francisco 39. Brunner lost a yard on a sack, but bounced up on the next play and completed a 10-yard pass to Young. Carpenter got the yard the Giants needed for the first down. The partisan crowd was growing edgy.

New York was threatening on the 29 yard line. Brunner was thinking 'pass' now. His first to Gray in the end zone was incomplete. Then he missed on a short strike to Bright. Looking at third and long, Brunner had to throw again. He fired in the direction of reserve wide receiver Johnny Mistler, who made a spectacular one-handed catch on the 11 yard line. The Giant drive that was seriously jeopardizing the 49ers' lead was still very much alive.

Bulldozing ahead, Carpenter busted up the middle for five yards. He tried it a second time and was held to two yards. The Giants faced a third down play, their biggest of the game. They decided on a pass. It was a quick one to Gray. Eric Wright was just as quick. He arrived to defend against Brunner's pass the same instant the ball reached Gray. Wright batted it away. Instead of a tying touchdown the Giants had to settle for a field goal. Danelo came in to line up a 21-yarder but kicked the ball wide.

The 49er offense couldn't rally. After Ring gained five yards and Montana flipped an 11-yard pass to Eason Ramson, the Niners stalled. Montana was forced to run out of the pocket to get two yards. Cooper was stopped with only a yard. On third down, Montana attempted to throw to Clark but was unsuccessful. With little over a minute remaining, Miller saved the 49ers with a 49 yard punt.

A clipping penalty on the kick positioned the ball on the New York nine. It was up to the Niners' defense to hold and elicit good field location from which the offense could strike. Carpenter could only reach the 10; Perry made it to the 11 as the third quarter play ended. The Giants were confronted with a key third down decision. They had to pass. Lott was thinking along the same lines. Brunner

threw to Perkins as the fourth period began. Lott stopped Perkins after a five-yard gain, leaving the Giants short of a first down by three yards. Jennings, pressured to kick, managed to boot a 42-yard punt to Solomon on the San Francisco 42. Eluding tacklers, the shifty Solomon returned the ball 22 yards before he was upended on the New York 36. San Francisco had excellent field position now.

It was up to Montana to capitalize on it. His first pass was incomplete, but the Giants were penalized three yards for pass interference, giving the Niners a first down on the 33. A pass to Ring lost four yards. On second down, the 49ers were penalized 10 yards for holding. They were strapped with a second and 24 on the 47 yard line. Somehow, they had to break loose.

Montana calmly tossed a six yard pass to Wilson. It seemed insignificant at the moment. However, an official, separating Gary Jeter and Dan Audick, who were fighting, penalized Jeter for unnecessary roughness. Suddenly the Niners had a first down on the 26. It was the opportunity they'd prayed for. Solomon scampered on a reverse for 12 yards to the 14. Ring kept it going with a seven-yard pick up around left end. Johnny Davis dove up the middle for four yards. The result: San Francisco had a first down on the three yard line. Ring didn't keep Niner fans in suspense. He slipped through a hole on the right side and scored standing up. Wershing's conversion pushed the 49ers' lead to 31-17. Jubilation reigned at Candlestick.

That touchdown rattled the Giants. They were ineffective following the kickoff. All three of Brunner's passes fell harmlessly to the ground. To make matters worse, they were slapped with a holding penalty on the 20 yard line. Jennings' 51-yard punt rolled dead on the 49ers' 29 yard line. San Francisco was only 9:46 away from victory.

Ring gained three yards; Cooper gained four. San Francisco now had a third and three on the 36. The Giants expected Montana to pass. Instead, Ring carried the ball, slipped around right end and cut back across the field for what appeared to be a fine 40-yard run. Unexpectedly, the Niners were penalized 15 yards for an illegal crackback by Wilson. The run being nullified, San Francisco had a third and long on their 21. Feeling the press of New York's pass rush, Montana scrambled out of the pocket and passed incomplete to Clark. Miller continued his sure-fire punting by hitting one for 52 yards. It went out of bounds on the New York 27.

The Giants couldn't advance on offense. Brunner tried three more passes—all three missed their mark. Once again, Jennings had to punt. There was 7:30 left in the game when the 49ers took over on their 35. All they needed to do at this point was to run out the clock. Walt Easley started by gaining three yards. Ring added two more before Easley ran straight ahead for five yards and a first down. Keeping on the ground to use up time, Easley got another yard. Ring got two more as the clock ticked along. They came up with a yard short on an end around as Clark got to the New York 46. There was only 4:21 left when Miller's punt went out of bounds on the New York nine yard line.

Willie Harper almost recorded a safety when he sacked Brunner on the one yard line. Remaining in the shotgun, Brunner tossed a six-yard pass to Perkins. The Giants still had 12 yards to go for a first down. Brunner tried to go for it, but his pass was intercepted on the 20 yard line by Lott, who ran it all the way back for a touchdown that sealed the Giants' doom. Wersching's conversion ballooned San Francisco's lead to 38-17. Only 3:11 showed on the clock. No one could convince 49er fans that the game wasn't over. It mattered not that the Giants managed to score another touchdown on Brunner's 17-yard pass to Perkins at 1:21 from the end. The final score stood at 38-24.

The 49ers seemed to take their triumph in stride. In retrospect they had to marvel at the effectiveness of several strategic innovations that Walsh had carefully designed for the game. One was the defensive maneuver that was so shattering to Giant linebacker Lawrence Taylor he refused to talk, even to his hometown reporters, after the game. In studying game films, Walsh had noticed that Taylor had no difficulty blitzing from his outside linebacking position. The reason was simple, the way Walsh saw it. A back, who had the responsibility for blocking Taylor in passing situations, could not handle the rookie's speed and strength. Conceding that, Walsh transferred that assignment to left guard John Ayers who handled Taylor easily.

Then, offensively, in order for the Giants' defense to respect the deep pass, Walsh added Pass 90 to the San Francisco playbook in his week-long preparations. In the second period, with the Niners holding a slim 10-7 lead, he unveiled his brainchild. It resulted in Montana throwing a 58-yard touchdown pass to Solomon that took the Giants completely by surprise.

"When Bill designed it at the beginning of the week, he said, 'Let them know it's a run; go after them and knock them on their butts,'" right guard Randy Cross told the press. "He told us not to worry about the sack. If a guy gets by, let Joe avoid him. It worked real well. I know one of the linemen came flying over me to hit Johnny Davis."

The play fooled the Giants and made them leary of the long pass for the rest of the afternoon. It was especially gratifying to Solomon, who had been sick with a virus before the game.

"It was just a 'go' pattern and I was able to get behind my man," explained Solomon. "Joe told me if the defender went for the play-fake, just to keep going. This was the first time since the early part of the season that I have been healthy. Up to now, I just tried to play hurt."

Walsh realized it, too.

"We knew he'd been ill, but we were counting on him doing everything he did," Walsh remarked. "One of the advantages we had today was that Freddie Solomon was healthier than he'd been for the previous game against New York. That game, we mainly used him as a foil. He only caught one pass. Our offensive execution was as good as I've seen with the 49ers. The offense won the game for us today. It was our best game to date this year. Joe played an exceptional game other than that one disastrous interception he threw."

Montana certainly had a great day. He completed 20 of 31 passes for a career high of 304 yards. He realized, though, how costly his interception in the third period might have been.

"I didn't want to happen what has happened to other teams that had big leads in the playoffs," Montana explained. "You don't want to make the big mistake. I should have thrown it away. We were faking screens and using a lot of play-action that was freezing the defensive backs. We wanted to get some respect or get some points and we got both. Throwing deep was important because we had to stretch their defense or their great linebackers would keep closing down tighter and tighter until they squeezed the life out of our offense. I think the big thing everybody was afraid of was our lack of playoff experience. Who knows, maybe our youthfulness is helping us instead of hurting. We're playing emotional football."

Another form of emotion served to be the Giants' undoing. Early in the fourth quarter with San Francisco's lead narrowed to 24-17, when the Giants appeared ready to get the ball again. At the time, the 49ers had not scored in 25 minutes of play. However, referee Ben Dreith called a personal foul on the Giants' Jeter for attempting to hit Dan Audick in the stomach after a play had ended with a six-yard 49er gain. The penalty gave San Francisco a first down, and four plays later the Niners scored to increase their lead to 31-17.

"I was blocking him, blocking him as long as I could under the rules," Audick explained. "I guess he felt it was too long and attempted to retaliate. He threw a blow to my stomach. He also yelled some obscenities at me. Then the official threw the flag and yelled a bunch of obscenities at him—nothing I would say in front of my mother."

It was frustration on Jeter's part. The Giants were trying to play catch-up football most of the game after Montana had rattled them with an overpowering first-half performance. Strong safety Bill Currier alluded to it.

"We couldn't allow them to neutralize us early and that's what happened," Currier claimed. "They had us thinking instead of reacting. They took away our aggressiveness and that really hurt. They ran plays that were not typical of the situation. Throwing it on first downs, running it when we thought they'd throw, reverse, quarterback draws. Most teams have tendencies. Their whole offense is based on not having tendencies."

Cross said that he heard all week how the Giants were prepared to neutralize the 49ers' offensive attack. In reality, San Francisco kept the Giants' defense off balance.

"I'd heard a quote on the radio from Scott Brunner on Saturday night that their defense was so good and how it should be able to stop our offense," Cross said. "I read a quote in the paper by Carpenter that said the 49ers can't compare in talent with the Giants. You're not going to win or lose football games with stuff like that, but you do definitely notice remarks like that. We go out of our way not to make comments like that. Most guys are psyched and crazy enough at the start of a game not to give them any additional edge.

"It may sound like I'm being redundant about Montana because it's been said about him so much this year. But, he's so cool under pressure. He gets hit occasionally very, very hard and it has very little effect on him. He throws a touchdown pass, he's happy. He doesn't throw a touchdown pass, he's not going to get depressed. He's not a Bert Jones yelling and screaming kind of guy. He's pretty unique, really. Capacity-wise, he's along the lines of a Jim Plunkett. He's pretty hard to shake up."

Jeter was still stunned as he prepared to leave the Giants' dressing room.

"Ask the referee, he called it," Jeter fumed. "I just hope Audick sleeps well tonight."

He certainly would. He had the Dallas Cowboys to dream about . . .

New York Giants		7	3	7	7	24
San Francisco 49ers		7	17	0	14	38

San Francisco: 5:57, first period—Young, 8-yard pass from Montana (Wersching, kick).
New York: 12:15, first period—Gray, 72-yard pass from Brunner (Danelo, kick).
San Francisco: 0:03, second period—Wersching, 22-yard field goal.
San Francisco: 2:56, second period—Solomon, 58-yard pass from Montana (Wersching, kick).
San Francisco: 4:36, second period—Patton, 25-yard run (Wersching, kick).
New York: 9:28, second period—Danelo, 48-yard field goal.
New York: 3:47, third period—Perkins, 59-yard pass from Brunner (Danelo, kick).
San Francisco: 4:23, fourth period—Ring, 3-yard run (Wersching, kick).
San Francisco: 11:49, fourth period—Lott, 20-yard interception return (Wersching, kick).
New York: 13:10, fourth period—Perkins, 17-yard pass from Brunner (Danelo, kick).

Fred Quillan gets set to pass block.

NFC CHAMPIONSHIP

The weather failed to improve and conditions worsened. Roads were being washed out and the Golden Gate bridge was closed for the third time in history. The ravage of floods had left an ugly scar on the surrounding countryside.

Through it all, Walsh and his players had ignored the elements in their determination to eliminate the New York Giants from the challenge for the Super Bowl. Now the forecast for even more rain caused Walsh real consternation. The NFC Championship game against the Dallas Cowboys was only six days away, and the coach believed it imperative that the team resume regular practice sessions (for the past week the team had been traveling by bus to different fields to work on dry turf). As Walsh explained at the time, "the fields here are so saturated we can't move around on them. We checked Fresno. We checked Santa Barbara. We've even talked of going as far as Tucson. But that's too dramatic a change."

He finally decided to try the Los Angeles Rams' training facilities in Anaheim, some 35 miles outside of Los Angeles. Much to their dismay, the rain that had splattered the 49ers for weeks seemed to follow them as they took the field in Anaheim on Tuesday. Still, it was more tolerable than what they had left.

Meanwhile, the weather in Dallas was like spring—ideal for practice. Cowboys' coach Tom Landry didn't want any part of the rain that was playing havoc with the 49ers' preparations. He planned to stay in Dallas as long as possible and not leave for San Francisco until Friday before the game. Even so, the players were nervous about the field conditions at Candlestick. Some had asked if they should work out in long cleats or in their regular practice shoes, and Landry worried that such thoughts might affect his players' concentration.

"If you start thinking that, it might be a disadvantage, what you think determines how you will play," he said. "Hopefully, we are experienced enough to just go out and play as hard as we can.

"Look, you play on a muddy field. You play in cold weather like we did in Green Bay. You just play. Both sides are cold, both sides are muddy, and both sides are slippery. You just hope when it's all over, you've had enough breaks to offset it. Breaks will make a big difference on a field that's not very good. We will just wear the longest cleats we can. You are

Dwight Clark leaps high and clutches the game-winning touchdown pass in the final seconds that put the 49ers into the Super Bowl.

limited in what you can do if the field is too slippery or too muddy. They have put a lot of sand on the field, so I would think it would not be like the type of field that say, Cleveland's can sometimes be. That field gets real heavy and I don't think we will have that in San Francisco."

Nevertheless, Landry was concerned. The Cowboys, who train on artificial turf, almost always perform better on that surface because their offense is designed around speed (particularly the quick bursts by halfback Tony Dorsett). A slow field could handicap a runner of Dorsett's speed and quickness.

"Obviously, with the softness of the field and the lack of traction, the stronger a guy is the less difference his power makes," Landry acknowledged. "Still, I think Dorsett will run well. He's a pretty good straight line runner. He's not the type to jitterbug all over the field. When he goes, he moves with acceleration, and therefore the field should not be a big factor."

Dorsett himself didn't appear too concerned. "I really don't know what the conditions are going to be and I figure if it's bad it's going to affect everybody. To a degree, a bad field would affect my cuts, and you've got to be careful how you run. But that's the least of our worries. Here in Dallas we don't give it any thought. We feel if we start worrying about a field, we're really detracting from ourselves."

Walsh looked at it differently. "I think there's a dramatic difference between Dallas' field and ours. If either club has to play on the other club's field, they are at a disadvantage. The synthetic surface at Texas Stadium is very, very fast. Dallas is used to it and built its club accordingly. It would have been brutal for our very, very young team to go down to Dallas to play."

What was more distressing for Landry and the Cowboys was the condition of defensive tackle John Dutton. He awoke with pain in his right thigh on Wednesday morning, five days before the game. Dutton had had trouble with his leg ever since Conrad Dobler of the Buffalo Bills had "leg whipped" him in a game at Dallas back on November 9. Dobler was penalized for unsportsmanlike conduct after Dutton had beaten him on a pass play. He

limped to the team's practice session later that morning and was driven to the offices of the team's doctor for a diagnosis. The team's trainer feared he had broken a blood vessel.

"I woke up about 5 o'clock, and it hurt like heck," said Dutton. "The swelling has gone down some, but when I first woke up it was pretty nasty. I sure couldn't run right now if I had to. I've never had anything like it before."

Landry knew Dutton's value to the Cowboys' defensive line and was worried that he might not be able to play.

"One of the big reasons we're a better team this year is because our defense has improved, and one of our most improved players is Dutton," said Landry. "The thing about defensive linemen is they play around people, and if they have confidence in those people, they play better. It would be very difficult if Dutton got hit on the leg again. He's very questionable.

The big tackle wasn't allowed to work for the remainder of the week and was ordered to rest and take treatments at the Cowboys' training compound. By the time the Cowboys arrived in San Francisco Friday night, it was clear Dutton couldn't play. Larry Bethea was named as his replacement. One of the main strengths of the Dallas team was now significantly weakened. Not only had Bethea been disappointing as the number-one draft choice of four years ago, but the Cowboys were lacking in reserves. The only other lineman they had available was Bruce Thornton, who still had a cast on his broken hand. There was no question that the Dallas pass rush, which had helped immensely in masking the deficiencies of a somewhat weak secondary, would be less effective than usual. With the exception of strong safety Charlie Waters, the Dallas secondary was almost as young and inexperienced as the 49ers'.

But the 49ers had also suffered an injury setback. Ricky Patton, who had hurt his leg against the Giants on Sunday, did not practice all week. Not only was Patton the team's leading ground-gainer, he was also valuable as a pass receiver. Walsh chose Lenvil Elliott to replace him. However, he kept the Cowboys alert by hinting that he wouldn't hesitate to use Patton in a spot play where he could utilize

Ronnie Lott and Willie Harper display joy after pass intended for Preston Pearson (88) was intercepted.

his skills.

There was no hiding the fact that the Cowboys had been hoping the Giants would beat the 49ers in the opening round of the playoffs. Had the Giants won, the NFC Championship game would have been played in Dallas. During the regular season the Cowboys had won all of the eight games that had been played in their own backyard. Yet on the road, Dallas' record had been mediocre. They split the eight games they played.

One of those losses was to San Francisco, on October 11. In fact, that defeat was the worst a Dallas team had suffered in a decade. The Cowboys had lost 45-14, and the 31-point embarrassment was the biggest since the St. Louis Cardinals routed Dallas 38-0 on national television in 1970. Cowboys president Tex Schramm had been in obvious pain when the fourth quarter of the San Francisco game began. Dallas was already far behind, 38-7, when the 49ers intercepted a pass and threatened to score yet another touchdown.

"If they score again, I'm going to need a large scotch," moaned Schramm.

Minutes later, Amos Lawrence scored from the one yard line. Shortly thereafter, a press box attendant appeared with Schramm's scotch.

Still, the Cowboys were established as 2½ point favorites over the young 49ers. The nation's oddsmakers felt that Dallas' playoff experience was a decisive factor. They also felt that the Cowboys would play with a vengeance after such a humbling defeat. They remembered what Dorsett had said earlier in the week:

"The 49ers humiliated us earlier in the year and we owe them one. What went wrong that day was that we showed up. We were just flat. We weren't ready mentally. We had a lack of respect for the 49ers then. We had beaten them 59-14 the year before. We figured it would probably be more of the same. I was flat along with everyone else. I was kind of lackadaisical. My performance was like everyone else's . . . bad.

"When you get beaten 45-14, if you don't respect a team, you're crazy. Besides, they didn't just beat us. They've got the best record in the NFL. Talent-wise, we're probably on the same level as some of our other Super Bowl teams. But emotionally, including some of those other intangibles, we're on a higher level."

"To be really honest," said defensive end Ed "Too Tall" Jones, "I didn't have a whole lot of respect for the 49ers before that game. I didn't think they could beat us regardless of what happened. I didn't know the names of half the team. Then things started happening so fast we couldn't get control of the game. Believe it or not, I still didn't have much respect for them when it was over, either. I never thought there would be a rematch in the playoffs. Even though they beat us that day, they didn't beat the real Cowboys.

"Look, all you have to do with Montana is throw his timing off and you blow his game. The Giants didn't pressure him at all. I noticed that he threw a lot of low passes in that game, and all of them were to my side of the field. If he does that this time, I'm going to get him. If I block a few early, look out."

"We're a better team than the one that played Philadelphia in this game last year," said Landry. "Our defense is better, especially in the secondary. It's all come together lately, but we'll probably give up 21 points. I don't know how you can stop the 49ers completely. They're going to score, but so are we.

"It's awfully tough for a good team to beat another good team twice in a row. The first-time loser has a lot of advantages, psychological and otherwise. Yet turnovers decide most playoff games. The psychology of concentration in a sudden death game is important. Once a player breaks his concentration and thinks about a mistake, like a turnover, then he's through.

"The game has changed. Not just the rules, but changes in defense with so many teams using three-man fronts. That helps rookies move in and play because of heavy uses of zone defense. In the old days if you had a rookie in there, he would be in man-to-man coverage a lot, and you could go at him. Nowadays, you can't isolate them that much."

In Dallas' opening playoff win, the Tampa Bay Buccaneers were buried under the pressure of the Cowboys' front four, 38-0. Their performance was so powerful that Jones, Dutton, tackle Randy White and end Harvey Martin were being referred to as "Doomsday II," in a comparison with the famed Dallas line of the late 1960s that was known and feared as the "Doomsday Defense." It would be up to the 49ers' offensive line to protect Montana from their onslaught.

Bobb McKittrick, San Francisco's line coach, knew they could do it. Center Fred Quillan, guards Randy Cross and John Ayers, and tackles Keith Fahnhorst and Dan Audick had protected Montana throughout the season and the nimble quarterback had been sacked only 26 times, or an average of 1.6 times per game. It is an impressive record considering that Montana attempted a total of 488 passes.

"The most impressive thing about this line's success is that it makes fewer mistakes than any line I've ever coached or seen on film," says McKittrick. "I guess you could call them over-achievers in that they get more out of themselves than one would normally expect. The key to their consistency is that, except for Audick, they have all been together for three years now, and they know each other.

"That is critical on an offensive line because one breakdown can cause a chain reaction that knocks down the whole wall, unless they know each other so well that if something does happen they react almost instinctively to compensate. I think we reached that stage this year.

"The tempo of our passing game helps, of course. We throw quickly and don't usually ask our guys to block all day like some teams do. But even considering that, these guys do a tremendous job. And in this game, they will be tested because, quick tempo or not, it is difficult to prevent Dallas' defensive linemen from harassing the quarterback. Their guys are so tall that it's not enough just to keep them off the quarterback. You can't let them penetrate more than a couple of steps or they'll obstruct Montana's view."

Before the 1981 season began, the 49ers' offensive linemen toiled in relative anonymity—until they raised eyebrows around the league by winning the Western Division title.

"Cross made the Pro Bowl this year and he has deserved it for a couple of seasons," says McKittrick. "Randy is the complete player.

There's nothing he can't do. He pass-protects well and is an excellent pulling guard. He has the ability to overpower or finesse a guy.

"Audick is the least physical lineman for his position. He might even be a little undersized for offensive tackle. He is quick, tough and might have the best nasty streak on the unit, which I kind of like.

"Quillan is an outstanding athlete with excellent feet. I just wish he would play consistently with more intensity. He feels he's at his best with a man over him in an odd front, but with his quick feet, I think he is just as effective against a 4-3 like what Dallas uses.

"Ayers is the quietest guy on the line. His strength is pass protection. He has uncanny balance because he keeps a good center of gravity. Some bigger tackles try to shake him around, but when they're done shaking, he's there in front of them.

"Finally, there is Fahnhorst. He is the biggest, the most physically imposing of the group. He is the prototype in size. This has been his best year because he has acquired a quiet confidence which he lacked."

There was no question that the outcome on Sunday, muddy field or not, was contingent upon the success of the San Francisco line against Dallas' front four. Nevertheless, even after studying the Dallas-Tampa Bay game film, in which it was obvious that the Cowboys' pass rush had destroyed Tampa quarterback Doug Williams, Walsh was optimistic.

"They will not do that," he vowed. "Not a chance. There's not much bravado in just saying that but our offensive line has been good and they stood up well the last time we played Dallas. Our two guards are as fine as any in the league. We put a lot of pressure on our line because we usually release our backs downfield as receivers. So the linemen are often caught blocking one-on-one without help.

"The Dallas defensive line is the key to the game. If they can really harass our quarterback and disrupt our timing, we'll be in trouble. But if we can protect Montana, then we'll have a good, high scoring game. It should be a great game. I see both clubs moving the ball awfully well—about 350 yards of offense for each. Four touchdowns will probably win it.

154

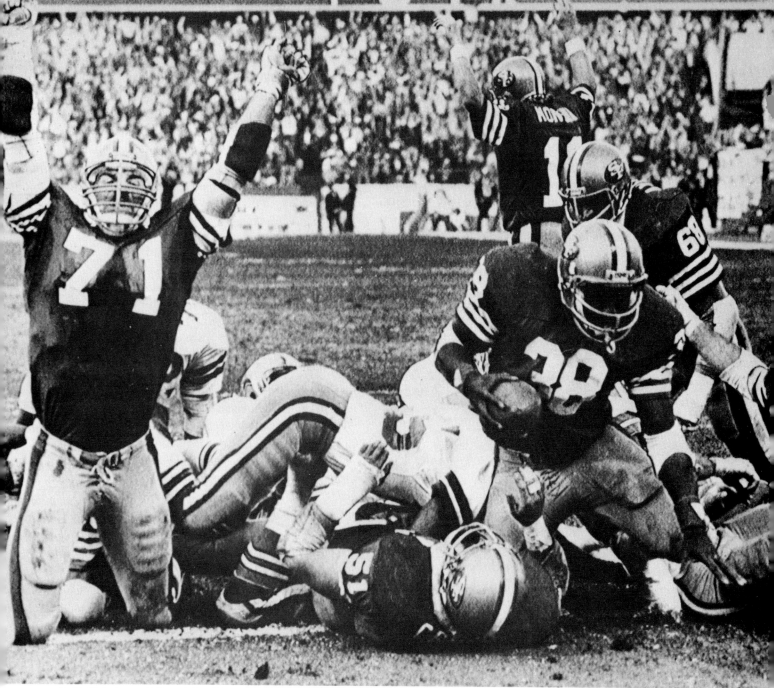

Keith Fahnhorst (71) and Joe Montana hold hands high to indicate that Johnny Davis (38) scored a touchdown.

We're young and they have the advantage of experience and they're bigger. We're faster, though, and we have the best record in the NFL. We've won 13 of our last 14 games and we're confident . ."

By week's end, the sun finally came out, bringing a smile to the face of John Wurm, the head groundskeeper at Candlestick, who had by now become almost as well known as the Golden Gate Bridge. Wurm had recently had his share of abuse from irate fans.

"You know, people around here don't know what they are talking about when they talk about bad fields," says Wurm. "I used to be head groundskeeper when the 49ers played at Kezar Stadium. You want to talk about mud? We had mud at Kezar. I remember one time when the Packers came in. Vince Lombardi's shoes got so buried in the mud, he walked right out of them." Ironically, sod from Kezar (a Hawaiian type known as Kakhua, which roots quickly) was used to repair the field at Candlestick.

"This is an Ed Podolak-type field," said Toma,

remembering the former running back of the Kansas City Chiefs, who wasn't known for his speed. "He liked it soft like this."

On Sunday, the warm sun shone brightly. The rain was gone. It turned out to be a perfect afternoon for football. The temperature reached 55 degrees and there was no wind. More than 60,000 title-hungry fans turned out for the game. Having won the coin toss, the Dallas captains elected to receive the opening kickoff. Ray Wersching teed up. At one minute after 2:00 he booted the ball toward Timmy Newsome. It went out of bounds but on the second kick Newsome caught the ball on the seven and returned it to the 26 yard line as the 49er defense came on the field for its first test.

Dorsett felt the effect of the soft ground right away when he tried to sweep around right end but was brought down after a two-yard advance. On second down, quarterback Danny White tried to complete a pass over the middle to tight end Doug Cosbie, but it was broken up by Jack Reynolds. White had the Cowboys set in a shotgun formation on third down. Dwaine Board was ready. He broke through from the right side and sacked White for an 11-yard loss on the 17 as the crowd roared. Dallas had to punt. Freddie Solomon then gathered in White's kick on the San Francisco 34 yard line and returned it for three yards.

Montana trotted out to join the offensive huddle as the fans applauded. On the first play he completed an 11-yard aerial to Mike Shumann. Then he tried a short pass to Elliott that missed, but a pitch out to Earl Cooper picked up three yards to the 49. On third down, Montana, looking for an open receiver, scrambled around and picked out Young, cutting across the field, for a 17-yard gain on the Dallas 32. The 49ers were in excellent position to score.

Montana passed again and Elliott broke out of the backfield to pull in the ball on the eight yard line. Niner fans felt a touchdown coming. So did Montana. He fired a quick sideline to Solomon, who sidestepped cornerback Dennis Thurman and fell into the end zone to score the first touchdown. Wersching added the conversion and with less than three minutes

gone, San Francisco was out in front 7-0.

Following the kickoff, Dallas put the ball in play on its 29 yard line. A quick pass to tight end Billy Joe DuPree earned five yards. Dorsett then skipped eight yards up the middle for a first down on the 42. A holding penalty set the Cowboys back ten yards, but Dorsett gained back five on a draw and added nine more on a sweep around the right side. On third and six White completed a 20-yard pass from the shotgun to Butch Johnson on the San Francisco 34. The Cowboys were beginning to stir. Archie Reese nailed James Jones for a two-yard loss. Jones then advanced six yards on a draw. On third down he caught a pass from White but could only gain three yards, leaving Dallas three yards short of a first. However, Rafael Septien got the Cowboys onto the board with a 44-yard field goal to trim San Francisco's edge to 7-3.

Starting on the 21 after the kickoff, Montana hit Young in the middle for an eight-yard gain to the 29. He tried to pass again, couldn't find an open receiver and finally threw incomplete in Solomon's direction. Trying to pick up the first down, Bill Ring was hit hard by linebacker Bob Breunig and fumbled, and Mike Hegman, the outside linebacker, pounced on the loose ball on the 29.

The turnover provided the Cowboys with an excellent scoring opportunity. Jones remained in the lineup as Dorsett was sidelined with an injured eye, from a finger that had gotten under his face mask the last time he ran with the ball. On first down, Jones moved for three yards. Then White stunned the crowd. On a timed sideline pattern, he delivered a 26-yard touchdown pass to Tony Hill who caught the ball on the goal line and stepped untouched into the end zone. Septien converted, and the Cowboys went in front, 10-7.

An illegal block on the kickoff put the Niners in a hole. They were lined up on the nine. They fell deeper in the hole when Elliott was dropped for a three-yard loss on the six. Finally Cooper broke through for six yards to give the 49ers a bit more room, and Montana faced a third and seven on the 12 yard line. Attempting a pass, he was pressured by the Cowboy defense and threw incomplete to Dwight Clark.

Joe Montana has that happy feeling after realizing that Dwight Clark caught a last second pass much to the chagrin of Dallas' Larry Bethea.

When Jim Miller entered the game for the first time, he had to kick from his own end zone with the Cowboys anticipating a prime field position. However, he got off a good punt to the Niner 49, where Jones caught the ball and returned it to the 36. With 1:33 remaining in the first period, the Cowboys returned on offense with an outstanding opportunity to increase their lead.

They went to the air. White's first pass fell incomplete. Then Willie Harper read a second down screen pass and dumped Ron Springs for a three-yard loss. The quarter came to an

end as White passed to Doug Donley, generating four yards, to the 35. Between periods Landry and White agreed to punt on fourth down, and when the second period began, White's punt landed in the end zone.

When the ball changed hands Cooper tried to run from the 20 yard line but was upended for a two-yard loss. Ring was successful, however, turning around the right side to run for 11 yards. Montana then aimed for a first down and got it with a snappy four-yard pass to Young. Cooper again carried on first down and this time got two yards to the 35. Then in

Ray Wersching kicks the important point that provided San Francisco with its 28-27 victory.

a flawless move on second down, Montana bootlegged off play action and surprised the Dallas defense with a 38-yard aerial to Clark on the Dallas 27. The Niners were almost close enough for a game-tying field goal now. Harvey Martin wasn't about to let it happen by sacking Montana for a five-yard loss on the next play. Unbowed, Montana then went to Clark again, this time for 10 yards to the 22. Now the Niners were in field goal range but on third and five, they decided to go for all of it instead. As Montana dropped to pass, 49er fans looked on with excitement. Then as Montana searched the end zone for Mike Wilson, Everson Walls swept in and intercepted the ball on the two yard line, crushing 49ers hopes for a touchdown.

Attention shifted to the Niner defense. If they could deny the Cowboys a first down they might be able to hold their attack location.

White kept the ball on first down and was stopped for no gain. On second down, Springs picked up one yard. Looking at a third and nine, White called for a sweep. Jones maneuvered for seven yards before being bounced out of bounds just short of the first down on the 10. Now it was White's turn to punt from the end zone. He delivered as Dwight Hicks signalled for a fair catch on the Dallas 47.

The 49ers lined up to attack. Cooper found a big hole up the middle and rumbled for 11 yards before he was dragged down. Montana timed a quick pass to Solomon for 12 yards and another first down on the 24 yard line. Montana was bringing the 49ers right back. Elliott ran to his right and got to the 20. Dallas braced for the pass. However, Montana, ducking under a heavy rush, saw Clark turn Dennis Thurman around in the end zone. Clark moved to the outside to sucker Thurman, then cut back toward the post where Montana's pass dropped into his hands for a touchdown. Wersching's conversion gave the Niners a 14-10 advantage.

There was 6:12 left in the half when Dallas got the kickoff and opened the action on the 20 yard line. Springs moved for three yards, Dorsett returned to action and made his presence felt with a six-yard burst. White then fired a short one to DuPree for three more yards and a first down on the 32, and Dorsett added four yards, to the 36. When the Cowboys decided to go deep, wide receiver Drew Pearson raced down the right sideline. White looked around and threw toward him. Ronnie Lott, who was playing Pearson close, reached up and intercepted, but the cheers faded as an official's flag signalled Lott for interference.

The infraction was costly as it gave Dallas the ball on the San Francisco 12 yard line. Hicks offered Lott solace as the rookie appeared stunned by the penalty. Dorsett hit the middle and got five yards. Reynolds stopped Springs on the five after a pick up of two yards. The 49ers' defense faced a troublesome down, third and three. Would the Cowboys pass or run? San Francisco was looking for the pass. However, White crossed them up. He handed the ball to Dorsett who raced around left end for a touchdown. Septien's kick gave the Cowboys a 17-14 lead.

There was only 2:30 showing on the clock as the ball was placed on the 20 yard line following the kickoff. Montana's first down pass to Cooper failed. Then Elliott ran for three yards as the two-minute warning was given. On third down, Jones broke through and sacked Montana for eight yards—back to the 15 yard line. Once again, Miller came through with a pressure punt. This time, though, Jones fumbled on the Dallas 48 and Amos Lawrence recovered the ball on the 42.

There was still time for the Niners to score. The scoreboard showed 1:45 left. Montana calmly went to work. Unable to find a receiver, he scrambled for a couple of yards. The Niners suddenly got a break when a holding penalty on the play gave San Francsico a first down on the 35. Cooper's five-yard gain was immediately voided by Clark's illegal crackback block and the 15-yard penalty pushed the Niners back to the 45. Reading pass, Martin roared in from his end position and sacked Montana, forcing a fumble, and Bethea recovered for Dallas on the San Francisco 48. Montana, who had been sacked an average of less than two times a game, had now been dumped three times in one half!

The Niners couldn't afford to let the Cowboys advance any further when Jim Stuckey sacked White for a seven yard loss. San Francisco's defense kept the pressure on by foiling a screen pass to Dorsett. Next, Lawrence Pillers charged in on White on third down and buried him for a 13-yard loss. White then followed up by recovering his own fumble on the Dallas 32. Now White had to punt. San Francisco would get one more chance to score before the half ended.

Hicks collected White's kick on the 28 and got it to the 37 before being tackled. Only 34 seconds remained as the 49ers went into their standard two-minute offense. Montana cranked up his arm. Could he beat the clock? He passed to Clark for seven yards. He then came right back to him, this time for 11 yards, to the Dallas 45. San Francisco called time out with just 11 seconds left. Montana threw for the third straight time and connected with Solomon for a 16-yard pass to the 29, but the final seconds ticked away before they could get off another play. Although they trailed at the half, 17-14, they had outgained the Cowboys by a total of 206 to 108 yards. They had more first downs—12 to seven—and Montana was clearly out-passing White, having completed 13 of 18 passes for 186 yards while White was eight of 11 for 75 yards.

The Niners received the kickoff and started the second half on the 25 yard line but didn't get far. Elliott made five yards and Cooper added three. However, Ring was stopped for a no gain and Miller had to punt. When the Cowboys got the ball on a fair catch on their 34, they couldn't generate any offense either. Dorsett made only six yards on two carries. When White was called for intentionally throwing away a third down pass, the Cowboys were penalized and sent back to their 23 yard line with a loss of down. Hicks then caught White's 39-yard punt and ran it back

12 yards to midfield.

Montana tried to catch the Dallas secondary by surprise by throwing deep on first down. He avoided Randy White's rush and threw long to Solomon but didn't connect. White's presence caused Montana to hurry his throw and he overthrew his receiver. Ring then scampered behind Quillan's block for nine yards and almost got away before the Dallas secondary caught him. On third down, Montana kept the ball himself and picked up two yards for a first down on the Dallas 39. A holding penalty set them back to the 49. Unruffled, Montana completed a 16-yard pass to Young and secured the first down with a six-yard toss to Cooper on the 27.

The 49ers were gaining momentum. Elliott gained four yards and Cooper got seven more for another first down on the 16 yard line. They were close enough for a shot at a game-tying field goal. They never got that chance. Montana's pass bounced off Elliott's hands and into the arms of Randy White, who was dropped immediately on the 13 yard line. The Niners wasted a golden opportunity.

Unexpectedly, White came out throwing. His first pass to Springs was incomplete. He tried again but this time the ball slid out of Springs' hands and was intercepted by Bobby Leopold. The young linebacker ran for five yards before he was brought down on the Dallas 13. The Niners now had another scoring opportunity. Pacing themselves, they reverted to their ground game. Ring led with a six-yard gain to the seven. Walt Easley punched out two more to the five. Ring got the ball again, but this time he was stopped after a one-yard gain on the four. The 49ers were one yard short of a first . With fourth down coming up they decided against the easy field goal that would have deadlocked the contest at 17-17, opting instead for the first down. Montana felt that he himself had the best chance of making it. He lunged behind the hard charge of center Fred Quillan for just short of a yard when a flag popped up. A hush fell over the stadium, then erupted into a roar when the Cowboys were penalized for offsides, giving the 49ers a first down on the two yard line. The Niners didn't wait to cash in. Hard-running Johnny Davis shot up the middle into the end zone for the touchdown and Wersching's conversion gave the 49ers a 21-17 edge.

Following the kickoff, with 5:44 remaining in the third quarter, Dallas resumed its attack from the 31 yard line. Dorsett was limited to four yards on two carries, but White managed to get a first down with a 10-yard pass to Jones on the 45. A short pass to Springs moved them up four yards. Then Dorsett was stopped after a one-yard gain. White, facing a third and five, had to throw. His pass to Johnson appeared to be incomplete when, for the second time, Lott was penalized for interference. Again Lott shook his head in disbelief. It was a damaging penalty, giving Dallas a first down on the San Francisco 12 yard line, but the third period ended as Dorsett was halted with no gain.

At the beginning of the final quarter White's first pass to DuPree got seven yards. His next, intended for Cosbie in the end zone, was broken up by Eric Wright. The 49ers' defense held the Cowboys back. Facing a fourth and three on the five yard line, the Cowboys elected to attempt a 22-yard field goal. Septien's aim was accurate. San Francisco's lead diminished to a single point, 21-20.

The 49ers' next possession was costly. From his own 19 yard line, Montana tried to hit Shuman. deep but overthrew him. Then he went to Solomon and connected with a 21-yard throw on the 40. On first down, Elliott got four yards around left end. Easley tried the middle and added four more, but was hit hard by Breunig and fumbled. Walls fell on the ball at midfield, giving the Cowboys another chance to move ahead.

Dorsett raced around left end for 11 yards. Then White passed to Springs for 12 more yards, giving Dallas another first down on the 27. Dorsett got the ball again and added six more yards, to the 21. Suddenly, White switched to the air. He rolled to his left as his line went to the right. The maneuver worked. Cosbie slipped down field and was all alone on the goal line to catch White's 21-yard pass for a touchdown. Septien's extra point gave Dallas a 27-21 lead.

Little more than ten minutes remained to play when San Francisco cranked its offense on the 17 yard line after Septien's kickoff. Montana tugged on his face mask. He was getting ready to throw. His first pass to Cooper was incomplete. He then looked for Clark and found him, for an 18-yard strike, on the 35. The next pass was for Solomon, who sped deep down the right sideline with Walls trailing him. Solomon didn't catch it. Instead, Walls intercepted on the 27 as the crowd moaned.

Now the San Francisco defense was determined to stop Dorsett. He got only two yards on two carries, but White, passing out of the shotgun to tight end Jay Saldi for nine yards, managed to get a first down on the 38. A screen pass to Jones gained four yards, and Dorsett slipped around the right side for five more. Springs just barely got the first down with a yard pick up to the 48. White went back to Dorsett. He racked up five yards on two carries, reaching the Niner 47. San Francisco's defense was confronted with a crucial third down play. White had to pass. True to form, San Francisco's Eric Wright succeeded in breaking up an intended completion to Donley. The defense checked the Cowboys. White had to punt and Solomon signalled for a fair catch, carefully squeezing the ball to his chest on the 11 yard line.

Distance was now more of a problem than time was. There was 4:54 left on the scoreboard but the 49ers had an 89-yard journey to the goal line. San Francisco fans were wild with anticipation. The entire season had come down to this final series of downs. San Francisco had to score a touchdown or else the entire season would be left on the soft turf of Candlestick. Nobody knew it more than Montana, the seemingly unflappable quarterback.

On the first down, Montana attempted a high percentage pass to Elliott and missed. Then Elliott carried up the middle for six yards. On third down, Montana passed to Solomon for six yards to the 23. It was a critical first down. Elliott shook loose around right end for 11 yards to the 34. Then he went the other way and picked up seven more. Trying for a first down, Montana passed to Elliott again and failed. The hard-working halfback then carried for four yards on the next play, which was enough for a first down. However, Dallas was offside on the play and was penalized five yards, which gave the Niners a

first down on the 46. Then Montana flipped a five yard pass to Cooper and reached the Dallas 49.

At the two-minute warning, Montana went over to talk to Walsh. The tension was mounting. When he returned the 49ers immediately took the Dallas defense by surprise. Montana called a reverse and Solomon turned it into a 14-yard gain. (Only Walsh would have called a play like that with so little time left.) Landry frowned on the sidelines obviously upset with himself for not being prepared for the play. The 49ers had a first down on the 35 when Montana threw a sideline pass to Clark for 10 yards and another first down on the 25. Then Montana called Solomon's number and completed a 12-yard pass on the 13. The 49ers called time out when the clock was stopped at 1:15.

At that point, Landry sent his linebackers into the game rather than staying with the nickel defense. Again Montana went to Solomon, but his pass in the end zone sailed over his receiver's head. Elliott swept left end for seven years to the six, crossing up Dallas, as the 49ers called time once more. Montana and Walsh conferred on the sidelines, carefully going over the crucial third down play. There wasn't any time for failure now. Fifty-eight seconds remained. In that last minute, with the crowd roaring, Montana barked the signals, took the snap and dropped to pass. The crowd rose to its feet. Pressured by Jones and linebacker D.D. Lewis, Montana rolled to his right. He was looking for Solomon, who couldn't get free. The end zone was in chaos as Montana turned to Clark. The resourceful Clark had first cut to his right, then reversed to his left, only to turn again and run back to his right near the back line of the end zone. As he was going down, Montana lofted a high pass to him. It seemed too high to catch—a throw-away pass. But Clark, straining, leaped higher than he ever had before, and grabbed onto the ball in mid-air. He landed on the ground and made certain his feet did not cross over the end zone line. The referee raised his arms in the air to signify a touchdown. The game was tied, 27-27 with 51 seconds remaining. Magnificently, Montana had taken the 49ers 89 yards in 13 plays. All eyes were on

Wersching now. His placement could put the Niners into the Super Bowl. The kick sailed effortlessly over the crossbars and San Francisco took the lead.

The kickoff put the Cowboys on their 25 yard line. White dropped to pass and threw accurately to Drew Pearson on the San Francisco 44. Wright miraculously grabbed Pearson by the jersey and knocked him to the ground. It was a game-saving play because there wasn't anyone in front of Pearson and if he had gotten loose, he could have scored a touchdown. The play had covered 31 yards and San Francisco's hard-fought lead was threatened by a potential field goal. Dallas requested a time out with 38 seconds. The Niners had to defend against the pass now, and better than they had all season. White faded back. He was under pressure without enough time to throw when Pillers grabbed him seven yards behind the line of scrimmage and jarred the ball loose. Stuckey recovered it and the game was as good as over. All Montana had to do was to sit on the ball for the final 30 seconds.

The 49er dressing room was bedlam. Ed DeBartolo shook his head in disbelief. He'd missed the final touchdown drive as he'd elbowed his way through the crowd trying to think of what he would say to the players in their defeat. Now, he was too proud for words.

"Before going down, I'd been on the deck outside our box leading the cheers," said DeBartolo. "Then it looked hopeless, just hopeless. I wanted to get to the locker room to commiserate."

Instead he celebrated. It was the most momentous victory in 49er history. Clark's catch is already a legend in San Francisco.

"I was the secondary receiver," Clark admitted. "Freddie was supposed to get the ball. It was the same play as the first touchdown, but they bottled Freddie up this time. I just slid along the back of the end zone until Joe saw me. He was getting ready to throw the ball away but then he saw me. He put it up high so I'd have a chance to get it if I could go high enough. I guess you can go as high as you need to win a championship game. The throw was high, just like it had to be. I didn't think Joe was going to get it off.

"The sliding part of it hadn't materialized for me, though. Usually, I run my hook and they come back with me. But this time they didn't. All I could think of was to get my feet down in bounds. Then I looked for a flag. I couldn't believe we scored, I was so worn out at that point. In the huddle before that play somebody said that this was going to be the big play. I don't think it's really sunk in yet."

"I was screaming for Dwight to catch it," said Solomon. "I'm sure he didn't hear me. On our first touchdown, the Cowboys all went for Dwight and left me open. On the last one, they all went for me and left him open."

Actually, Solomon might have caught the winning pass three plays earlier if Montana's throw had been more accurate.

"He was open and I overthrew him," Montana confessed. "I was hoping that wouldn't be the only chance I got."

Later, when he described the winning touchdown pass, he said, "I didn't see the play until I saw it on TV in the locker room. It was about the most beautiful thing I've ever seen. We line up Freddie Solomon in the slot to the right and Dwight Clark about six years wide outside of him. As I roll to the right, Freddie runs a short pattern out to the right. Dwight is supposed to screen for him as he drives straight to the back of the end zone. If Freddie gets jammed, I look for Dwight. I was supposed to look for Fred, look for Dwight, and then throw the ball away. I don't know about luck. I just know where we're headed . . ."

Dallas Cowboys	10	7	0	10	27
San Francisco 49ers	7	7	7	7	28

San Francisco: 4:19, first period—Solomon 8-yard pass from Montana (Wersching, kick)

Dallas: 10:16, first period—Septien 44-yard field goal

Dallas: 12:11, first period—Hill 26-yard pass from White (Septien, kick)

San Francisco: 8:48, second period—Clark 20-yard pass from Montana (Wersching, kick)

Dallas: 12:30, second period—Dorsett 5-yard run (Septien, kick)

San Francisco: 9:16, third period—Davis 2-yard run (Wersching, kick)

Dallas: 0:52, fourth period—Septien 22-yard field goal

Dallas: 4:19, fourth period—Cosbie 21-yard pass from White (Septien, kick)

San Francisco: 14:09, fourth period—Clark 6-yard pass from Montana (Wersching, kick)

Cowboy quarterback Danny White fumbles near the game's end after being hit by Lawrence Pillers.

SUPER BOWL XVI

The Super Bowl had a special meaning for Bill Walsh, a deep, personal significance that extended over the years. Although he seemed calm, he quivered inwardly because of his background with Paul Brown, owner of the Cincinnati Bengals. The rancor of his final year as Cincinnati's quarterback coach had left Walsh with a queasy feeling that had lingered over the years. He had never fully expected to return to the National Football League as a head coach. Now, in only three years, he had coached his team into the biggest game of them all. It was also Cincinnati's first Super Bowl appearance, and it gave Walsh a measure of satisfaction that his team had made it in far less time than the Bengals, who, over the years, had loaded up with many number one draft choices.

A fiercely proud individual, Paul Brown is also vengeful. He doesn't forget anything or anybody who crosses him. Players like Bill Bergey and Bob Trumpy, even Blanton Collier, a former coach, had felt the wrath of Brown. When Cleveland owner Art Modell dismissed Brown as coach of the Browns in 1963, he offered the job to Collier, who had been an assistant coach for 17 years. Before accepting the job, Collier told Modell that he

would like to talk to Brown first. Brown told him to take the position. But Brown hasn't spoken to Collier since.

Walsh knew the feeling well. He had suffered similar indignities. Several days after San Francisco defeated Dallas for the NFC crown, Brown had been saying that he'd given Walsh his first start as a coach in the NFL, that he'd brought him up from a semi-pro team in California. He also mentioned that he had pulled Chuck Studley, Walsh's assistant, off a used car lot to give him a job with the Bengals. Brown's barbs did not set well.

"Walsh called me a couple of days after the Dallas game and told me what Brown had been saying," Al Davis, the owner of the neighboring Oakland Raiders said. "He asked me what to do about it. I told him just to ignore him; that's the way Brown is. He's just trying to play with your head."

Although he wasn't visibly upset, that was the hidden concern that followed Walsh to Detroit. Naturally, the press made references to his dislike for Brown. He handled the questions like the gentleman that he is, although he held back on his answers at times. Still, one could read between the lines.

"It's natural that the Paul Brown thing

would come up," Walsh said. "I wouldn't be here today if it wasn't for Paul Brown. Of course, that's a double-edged remark. I felt I was a craftsman and I was disappointed that I hadn't become a head coach sooner. I served as an assistant coach for many many years to the point where I wasn't awed by the hype and acclaim I've gotten. If I were ten years younger I might be a little more impressed. This moment came late for me."

What Walsh did do was to arrive in Detroit ahead of his team, ahead of everybody. He came alone after stopping in Washington to receive a Coach of the Year award on Saturday night. Although the league rules called for the team to appear at the Super Bowl site on a Monday, Walsh didn't fully subscribe to the edict. Instead, he brought his team in a day earlier, on Sunday. It was the first time that a competing team arrived so early since the New York Jets landed in Ft. Lauderdale ten days ahead of time for Super Bowl III in 1969.

Perhaps Walsh felt his players would be a little looser for the approaching week-long blitz by the media by arriving earlier. He certainly was thinking along those lines when he met the players' busses disguised as a bellman, uniform and all. He went unrecognized at first. Then the players broke up at the puckish act.

The 49ers found a dusting of snow on the ground, having just missed a moderate snowfall on Detroit and its environs earlier in the week. And it was cold. The temperature had fallen to 15 degrees below zero, a record low. A wind chill factor of minus 51 degrees made it feel even colder. The only comforting thought as the players bundled up was that the game on Sunday would be played indoors where wind and cold would not be a factor.

The one problem that Walsh had was the practice time that his team had been allotted. He made his feelings known, too, and he had a valid point. Earlier in the week, he had lost a coin toss with opposing Cincinnati coach Forrest Gregg to determine when their respective squads would practice, either in the morning or the afternoon. Since the 49ers were entering a three hour time zone differential, it meant that their practice sessions would, in reality, be at 7:30 in the morning. Walsh

"Bellman" Bill Walsh.

didn't like the arrangement at all. He didn't feel something as important as workouts, especially for a team from the west coast, should be decided by a toss of the coin. He hoped the situation would be rectified in the future, emphasizing that the press interviews scheduled for the players at 8:30 A.M. translated into 5:30 A.M. San Francisco time.

"I think the first consideration should be given the team that has to travel in from a different time zone," Walsh said. "We'll have to practice at 10:30 in the morning, which is like 7:30 our time. We'll have to get up at 5:30 our time. I'm not sure there was enough anticipation of these possibilities. Frankly, I'm not excited about that kind of treatment. But we'll deal with any adversity. We won't be able to follow a normal sequence of time—meeting, lecturing, that type of thing. This week is very important to us."

On the other hand, Gregg was delighted. It was like scoring the first points in a football game. He wanted the afternoon workout session for his team. He felt he'd gotten the psychological edge.

"I'm elated," Gregg admitted. "By working in the afternoon, it keeps us in the same schedule we're on now. I was hoping for this."

Walsh was also hoping that his strategies could diffuse the effectiveness of Bengal quarterback Ken Anderson, his former pupil.

Walsh had a high opinion of Anderson, who had enjoyed the finest season of his eleven year career. During the last two weeks in Redwood City, Walsh had studied Anderson hour after hour on film. Anderson was every bit as good as he was when Walsh had tutored him. Walsh's film ratings on Anderson were high. He detected the confidence that Anderson displayed with his passing and his scrambling. Fearless as a runner, Anderson had scrambled for 320 yards, the highest yardage on the Bengals behind their punishing fullback Pete Johnson. After seeing enough of Anderson on film, Walsh ordered his defensive coordinator Chuck Studley to work on exerting more pressure on the veteran quarterback—something new that the 49ers had never shown before in their games.

"Anderson's running is the key to the game for us," Walsh analyzed. "We've got to hit Anderson low, because he's very adept at getting underneath tacklers. He is the greatest runner at that position who's ever played. He gives Cincinnati a dimension that other people just don't have. Anderson is very fast. The only people who can stay with him are defensive backs. He is a great athlete.

"The other problem is to stop Johnson. He has dominated every game they played. My suspicion is that he will be their primary runner. They go out and get a lead and then Pete goes ahead and holds it. The only break we got when we played them earlier was we got ahead early and so they couldn't afford to let him keep running the ball."

When the 49ers had defeated the Bengals, 21-3, the first weekend in December, the burly 250 pound Johnson carried the ball only a dozen times. Still, he rushed for 86 yards, an average of a little more than seven yards a carry. No other runner did that well against the Niners all year. He was a major problem for the Niner defense.

"I don't foresee us being able to stop Johnson unless we get line penetration to make him run east and west so we can tackle him before he gets started," linebacker Willie Harper pointed out. "Once he turns north or south, he'll be a problem. He is a brute."

Ronnie Lott, the Niners' hard-hitting cornerback, wasn't looking forward to meeting Johnson in the open field, even though the star rookie is solidly built at 200 pounds. There aren't many cornerbacks around with that weight.

"To bring down Johnson by yourself, could be rough," Lott said. "It could take a toll on you. If he's in the secondary that much, you know it will be a long day for us."

The one thing that puzzled the experts was why it had taken so long for Cincinnati to reach the Super Bowl. For years, experts considered them to have the best talent in the league. The prevailing opinion was that Cincinnati was good enough to win the AFC in 1980, yet didn't. They did it in 1981 with only a few personnel changes, and they've had just about the best players in the AFC ever since Pittsburgh's draft selection began going bad.

Now, the Bengals had eight first-round draft picks in their starting lineup. In the 22 starting spots, there were no fewer than 16 first, second and third round draft picks. The

Dwight Clark boards the 49er Liner to Super Bowl XVI in Detroit.

167

Joe Montana calmly meets the press.

team was rich in talent.

"Everyone in football knew the Bengals had been developing into a strong team with high draft choices," Walsh observed. "We knew at one point it would all jell and overnight they would become the best team in their division. Pittsburgh knew it and Cleveland knew it, and I believe Cincinnati is here to stay."

During the 49ers' visit to Detroit for the biggest game in the club's history, Walsh decided to have as relaxed an atmosphere as possible. He set the tempo when the team arrived on Sunday. The curfew he imposed was midnight, which was quite generous. He also allowed the players to eat by themselves whenever they liked. The regimen was a stark contrast to the one programmed by his friend Dick Vermeil of the Philadelphia Eagles the year before in New Orleans. Vermeil did everything on a team basis. He even had the players eating together as a team every evening. He didn't allow them any time to relax, and the players grew tense by the time they appeared on the field against the Oakland Raiders, who defeated them quite easily,

27-10.

Alan Page, the former great Minnesota Vikings' defensive tackle, agreed with Walsh's approach. He was in Detroit for the game, his first time as an ex-player after ending his career with the Chicago Bears in December. Page appeared in four Super Bowl games with Minnesota but never came away with a ring.

"We were locked up all four times and the results speak for themselves," Page said. "What it does is isolate you from the rest of the world. It literally forces you to think about the upcoming game 24 hours a day. There is no escaping, no getting away to be by yourself. The parties and the hype are all part of the atmosphere. you can't be a part of it, but you feel the energy, the tension, the excitement. With that layered on top of your own energy, tension and excitement, you end up the end of the week just a bundle of nerves."

Joe Kapp agreed with his former teammate. Kapp had been the quarterback in Minnesota's first Super Bowl appearance against the Kansas City Chiefs in 1970, and now is the head coach at the University of California in

168

Berkeley.

"The Vikings were free-swinging free spirits," Kapp said. "We got caught up in the Super Bowl atmosphere and didn't keep our true personality. We went at it like it was work when the game of football should be fun. That's the way the 49ers play it now and the way the Steelers did when they were winning Super Bowls. It's the way Billy Martin's baseball teams play. I always said it was a game. Sure, it's our business, but there are people hungry in the world and there are poor people in this country. Coaches act like it's everything, but there's a real world out there."

Another former player, Andy Russell, a star linebacker with the Steelers, recalled his Super Bowl experiences. He was fortunate to play on two winning teams before retiring. The first one was against Minnesota in New Orleans in 1975.

"Chuck Noll told us to get New Orleans out of our systems," Russell recalled. "By Wednesday, we were begging for bedchecks. He told us before we got to New Orleans about the media crunch: 'Don't try to fight it; it's something you're going to have to do anyway so enjoy it.' Sometimes I get bored by all the same questions. Some of us played games with the press. Each player had a table for press interviews and I left mine to sit with Ray Mansfield. We started telling war stories; how Buddy Parker once cut 13 guys on a team plane before we got home; or how in training camp he woke up a trainer in the middle of the night to have him wrap up his hands like a prizefighter because he was going to fight the players. By the end, nobody was sitting with Joe Greene or Franco Harris or Terry Bradshaw. When the interview time was up, the writers started to leave and Mansfield yelled, 'come back, we're not finished.' It was the exact reverse of what it was supposed to be.

"Noll's pre-game speech certainly had to be one of the shortest. He told us; 'let's go out and have some fun.' Everybody just looked at each other. Frankly, I was having a hard time breathing. Both teams came out the same runway in New Orleans. I remember the Vikings were standing next to us. They all had their game faces on. I waved to a couple of guys I knew, but they wouldn't wave back. Our guys, meanwhile, had cameras and were taking pictures. The contrast was staggering. The danger is to be too psyched up, never the other way. You don't need to psyche up a team for the Super Bowl."

Apparently, Gregg didn't see it that way. The Cincinnati coach, who played under Vince Lombardi at Green Bay as a member of two winning Super Bowl teams, is a strict disciplinarian. Like Paul Brown, he won't deviate from his schedule. When the Bengals arrived in Detroit he left a busload of writers with empty note pads. The press had arrived at the Bengals' hotel expecting to interview the players. Gregg wouldn't allow it.

Before the team left Cincinnati, Fran Connors, the AFC's public relations director, had scheduled a press conference. Or so he thought. But shortly after the Bengals' plane landed in Detroit, Gregg informed the NFL offices that he had no intention of subjecting his players to a press conference the first day they arrived.

"We had set it up. We thought we could do it," acknowledged Cincinnati's public relations director, Al Heim. "Then on the way here, he decided not to."

Embarrassed, Connors tried to intercept the press bus and call off the conference, but was too late. To save further embarrassment, Connors and Heim prevailed upon Gregg to at least appear before the disgruntled writers. He finally agreed, but he didn't win any friends by making it clear he preferred to be somewhere else. He emphasized that he wouldn't tolerate any distractions when his team has a game to play, and that he can take the press in small doses but he's not going to swig it down.

"I love ice cream, but if I had to eat ice cream every day, I might get my fill of it," Gregg snapped. "I've about had my fill of ice cream."

Meanwhile, Hacksaw Reynolds couldn't get enough time viewing the game films on the projector he brought with him from San Francisco. He thought nothing of spending hours in the dark, alone, studying the Bengals, trying to break them down.

"They're a very hard team," Reynolds dis-

Coach Bill Walsh checks out the Silverdome.

closed. "They repeat a lot of the same plays, but in different situations and from different looks. It's hard to get a pattern on the beat of this team. They do things you least expect when you least expect it. The key for both of us is to keep our own offense on the field. Both offenses are really sophisticated and have a lot of weapons. As an example, if you key on Pete Johnson, they'll pass you silly; and now they're using Charles Alexander a lot more. He's a great runner, too.

"They also have great receivers, and they've got Ken Anderson and that Sherman tank Johnson back there. It's like having a guard or a tackle in the backfield. You can't tackle him with an arm or he'll tear your arm right off."

Reynolds also prepared for the press. For 13 years he had had to repeat time and again how he'd acquired the nickname, 'Hacksaw'.

Somehow, Reynolds' explanation never was written accurately. To avoid errors and having to repeat the story hundreds more times, Reynolds prudently had Delia Newland, one of the 49ers public relations aides, mimeograph the accurate version. He simply handed out hundreds of copies. For Super Bowl trivia buffs, it was a first. The official Reynolds' version:

"In 1969, when I was a senior at the University of Tennessee, we had already clinched the Southeastern Conference title but still had to play Ol' Miss where Archie Manning was quarterback. If Tennessee won the game, we would have gone to the Sugar Bowl.

"The previous year, Tennessee had beaten Ol' Miss, 31-0. Things went badly that day and Ol' Miss beat the Vols, 38-0. I played a good game and was really upset at the outcome, so I

170

went back to school.

"We had an old car, a '53 Chevrolet with no motor, on top of a bluff above the school. We used to push it around with a guy's jeep and practice driving into things, like demolition derby. When I got back to school I decided I would cut that old car in half to make a trailer for a new jeep I had just purchased. It was a good outlet for my frustrations.

"I went to K-Mart and bought the cheapest hacksaw they had, along with 13 replacement blades. I cut through the entire frame and drive shaft, all the way through the car. I started on Sunday and finished Monday afternoon. It took me eight hours total time. I broke all 13 blades. When I finished I went and got one guy from the dorm, Ray Nettles, to witness it. The next day we took the rest of our friends from the dorm up the hill to see it. And when we got there, both halves of the car were gone, with just the 13 broken blades lying on the ground. To this day, I don't know what happened to the car."

The weather was a great concern. The thought of snow sent a chill through NFL officials. Since this was the first Super Bowl game in sixteen years ever played outside the sun belt, the fear of snow hung like the sword of Damocles over the head of Jim Steeg, the league's director of special events. Steeg had been in Detroit since January 3, three weeks before Super Sunday. Besides worrying about the weather, Steeg also had to coordinate hotel lodging, transportation and training facilities.

Hotel accomodations weren't a problem. Neither was the training site, since both teams shared the Silverdome. Organizing the busses and trains for transportation were the challenge, since various groups were scattered around the metropolitan Detroit area. The press was quartered in Dearborn, the 49ers were in Southfield, the Bengals were in Troy and the Silverdome was in Pontiac. Steeg was armed with dozens of road maps.

For the first time, the NFL installed a National Weather Service wire report in its headquarters at the Hyatt Regency in Dearborn. They kept a close watch on the weather, beginning with three-day forecasts, which would be updated to three-hour outlooks should the threat of snow increase. It appeared as if the NFL was mounting a winter offensive. They marked the eight major routes to the Silverdome. Every piece of snow removal equipment was put on alert along the way. The drivers of the vehicles were ordered to be in their trucks from 10 A.M. until 8 P.M. on game day, regardless of whether it was snowing or not. They would operate under a special color code: Black Condition if the forecast was for two or more inches of snow and Red Condition if the prediction is less than two inches. As an extra precaution, 500 tons of salt was piled up at Oakland County Community College several miles from the stadium.

Steeg studied his history well. He went back 25 years to analyze the weather conditions in the area. He felt reasonably certain that it wouldn't snow.

"The real snow belt is 100 miles to the north," Steeg reported. "The bigger worry is a freezing ice storm. If it does happen to snow heavily, we could clear the roads, but not the parking lot."

As is always the case with a Super Bowl, the glut of ticket scalpers presents a problem. The situation fell under the investigation of Warren Welsh, the NFL's director of security. He had to meet several times with Detroit police to discuss the situation. Ticket scalping is illegal in Michigan.

"So far this year, we've heard of a dozen or so cases of scalping Super Bowl tickets in California, New York and elsewhere," Walsh revealed. "We're investigating the scalping with the Detroit police and other authorities in Michigan. We're hopeful something can be done to stop this. It's a very, very frustrating thing."

The scalpers were asking a big price. Since scalping is legal in California, some ticket brokers were anticipating a windfall. One broker took out an advertisement in a newspaper that included a toll-free telephone number for anyone wishing to sell Super Bowl tickets. They were willing to pay up to $200 for the $40 ticket. That was only the beginning. The broker in turn would resell the coveted ducat at prices scaled from $450 for a seat at midfield to $225 for one in the end zone.

Actually, the event was attracting more attention than usual. Since neither of the teams had been expected to be the contenders, the Super Bowl took on the appearance of a Cinderella Bowl. Both the 49ers and the Bengals were coming off 6-10 seasons the previous year. The improbability of the two reaching the Super Bowl had led the nation's bookmakers to establish them as longshots. Before the 1981 season began, the odds on Cincinnati were 70-1 while San Francisco was tabbed at 50-1.

The game itself was considered to be close. The 49ers had defeated the Bengals 21-3 during the regular season, and they were established as slight favorites to win a second time. The official Las Vegas betting line made San Francisco a slim one-point favorite. It opened at those numbers ten days before the game, and never fluctuated to any appreciable degree. It was the closest point spread in nine years. San Francisco was the sentimental favorite. But most of the NFL experts picked the Bengals to prevail. In a poll conducted a week before the game, 15 of the 21 NFL coaches liked the Bengals.

The Bengals faction was led by Dallas coach Tom Landry, still shaken by the nightmare of not being in the Super Bowl. Landry liked the Bengals by seven points.

"I'm not very good at picking games, but I'd have to go with Cincinnati and Anderson because of their experience," Landry observed. "Yet, the 49ers with all their inexperience don't seem to be bothered by the big games. The turnovers will be important. If Cincinnati can stay clear of turnovers, they'll win."

Ray Perkins of the New York Giants was even more convinced. He was generous in picking Cincinnati by ten points. Perhaps he was still smarting over his team's loss to the Niners in the opening round of the playoffs.

"I give the edge to Cincinnati simply because they have the more experienced quarterback," Perkins said. "If you look back over most of the Super Bowls, the teams whose quarterbacks have had the best days are the teams that have won."

Cleveland coach Sam Rutigliano was more expansive in his evaluation. The Browns were the only team to defeat both the 49ers and the Bengals during the regular season.

"Dan Ross and Pete Johnson are the keys to the Bengal offense, plus Anderson's great scrambling ability," Rutigliano began. "They try to get the ball inside to Ross early, and that opens up things deeper. Johnson is very effective as a lay-off receiver, and Anderson will go to that right away. You coach your ends to get containment on Anderson, to keep him from scrambling; but when your ends are worried about containment, their pass rush is limited. The rush must come from the inside. Montana is very similar. He'll dodge an outside rush. Both he and Anderson have great patience, waiting for their receivers to get open.

"The danger against San Francisco is to get impatient on defense, to come apart while the 49ers are piling up first downs. You have to concede them first downs. You have to close on their receivers and hold the gains to a minimum. And you have to play a lot of zone underneath and force them into third-and-short situations because the running game is the weakness in their offense."

As far as Dallas safety Charlie Waters was concerned, the 49ers' weakness is negligible. He was impressed by San Francisco's passing game, which is what got them that far to begin with. Waters and everyone else knows that Walsh isn't afraid to pass, no matter what the situation is during a game. The Super Bowl would not be an exception to Walsh's way of thinking, either.

"The 49ers' passing game is based on a series of picks that get their receivers free," Waters said. "Everybody uses picks, but not as intelligently as they do. There are some things they do that are almost sandlot. Those plays where Dwight Clark starts off one way and then, if he's covered, does a 180 degree turn and comes back. But you can tell they've worked on them a lot, because there's never any confusion there.

"That's the big thing that amazes me about their system. With all the new things that Walsh puts in every week, there's never any confusion. I want to get into coaching, and I'm going to ask Walsh if I can spend some time with him trying to learn his system."

It was the 49ers' adroit use of picks that rankled Hank Bullough, the Bengals' defensive coordinator. He wasn't upset about the

Fred Solomon and Dwight Clark take time out for the photographers.

picks the first time the Bengals lost to the Niners. The Niners hadn't used them at all. Rather, it was the application of them in the Dallas game, which Waters had spoken about, that had Bullough complaining first to Paul Brown and now to everyone.

"I expect Paul Brown to talk to the league office about it," Bullough fumed. "What happened in our game was that they got the lead on us early and controlled the game with their short passing game. They didn't have to do anything fancy in that one. Where the pick is most dangerous to a defense is close to the goal line. There are a lot of people in a small area of the field and it's easy for players to bump into one another.

"I couldn't believe what I read in *Sports Illustrated* when Walsh and his players were saying right in print they were using illegal plays. I mean, what the heck. Pick plays in this league are illegal, and here they are talking about the different types of pick plays they were using. I think the league should make the officials in the Super Bowl aware of this and make sure

they don't get away with it.

"In the article, they talked about this pick play and having a semi-pick play. I guess the semi-pick play is the one where you just brush the defender rather then running right into him. Other teams use the pick but they are smart enough to call it a different name. Some call it a cherry or an apple. Like you have to pick cherries or oranges, right?

"But those San Francisco people were just coming right out in print and saying they were using picks. Actually, I was glad to read it. It was so good. I read it a couple of times just to make sure. I even went out and got me another copy of the magazine to make sure they all said the same thing."

While Bullough was fretting about pass patterns with picks, San Francisco style, the 49ers were busily concentrating on honing their skills for a game that was considered to be a wide-open affair. The bulk of their preparations had been conducted in Redwood City the week before. During that period, Walsh had given Studley the assignment of figuring out a

Montana looks for a receiver.

way to exert more pressure on Anderson from the inside. Studley devised the Nickel Blizzard, which the 49ers hadn't used before. To execute it effectively, Carlton Williamson would blitz from his safety position.

In an effort to apply even more pressure to Anderson from the inside, Studley reached back into the past for another idea that the Oakland Raiders had employed with success. The Raiders had used Dan Birdwell, a bruising tackle, to move up and down the line looking for an open pass rush lane. The maneuver created havoc on opposing quarterbacks.

Studley took that concept and altered it. He placed three down linemen in the middle to pressure the guards and center. Next, he positioned two outside linebackers, Keena

Turner and Bobby Leopold, as down linemen also to protect against any scrambles Anderson might do. This allowed Fred Dean to roam along the line and charge from whatever lane he found open.

"Fred's eyes lit up when I showed it to him," Studley said. "I said, 'Give me a name for it; something with real impact.' 'Cobra,' Fred said. 'Call it Cobra.' "

Dean was a prime concern for the Bengals. In a classic one-on-one match-up he would, in most cases, go against the Bengals' behemoth tackle, 6'6", 278 pound Anthony Munoz. Dean was giving away four inches and 48 pounds. He had to rely on his quickness more than ever.

"Munoz is big and strong and has good

174

technique," Dean said. "When you play against a guy like that, you have to get him off balance and use his strength against him. If Munoz doesn't stop me, I'll be on Anderson all day. I don't feel I had a bad game the first time I played against him this year. My game was all right but I didn't feel it was as good as I wanted it to be. It could have been better. I was bothered by a bruised sternum, but that's not bothering me now."

Obviously, Munoz respected Dean. Professionals usually do.

"It is going to be tough, not only as far as combating his quickness, but his strength," Munoz said. "He's a tremendous athlete. I see it as playing against the best. It's a challenge. I think that helps me improve. I felt I did decently the last game against him. I wasn't too excited about it. I felt I could still be better. I don't think he got a sack, but he got close. I'll just try everything I can to slow him up on Sunday. It's a matter of watching films, seeing what his tendencies are. He tries to beat you on the tremendous quickness and speed he has. A lot depends on my technique."

Walsh never stopped innovating the entire week. He kept doodling with his Xs and Os, adding a play here and another there. He slipped about a dozen new plays in to the 49ers' playbook. Even the day before the game itself, Walsh inserted a new formation, an unbalanced line, that he wanted to use in short yardage situations. None of it surprised his players. Walsh had been doing this sort of stuff all season long.

Walsh never stops thinking. When the 49ers opened the 1981 season with a loss to the Detroit Lions, Walsh remembered the difficulty his team had fielding kickoffs. The Silverdome's artificial surface is hard, perhaps one of the hardest playing fields in the NFL. Walsh discovered, much to his chagrin in the opening game of the year, just how hard it truly was. The ball was extremely difficult to control after it hit the cement-like surface. What happened was that the football would ricochet like a cue ball off the side of a billiard table. Walsh never forgot that.

All week long, during the 49ers' final preparations for the Super Bowl, he instructed his veteran kicker, Ray Wersching, how to kick, or

more accurately, which way to do so. Instead of the conventional high, deep kicks needed to allow time for coverage by speedy *kamikaze* specialists, Walsh ordered Wersching to try to boom a line drive type of kick: not just any line drive kick, but one that would be skillfully positioned just over the heads of the second line of blockers. This would make the ball bounce well in front of the kick return experts, who run with the speed of a jaguar once they have their arms wrapped around the pigskin. Walsh was thoroughly convinced that the play would work successfully since the ball would take an erratic bounce and could not be handled with dexterity.

Walsh also turned to one more lesson in his Super Bowl playbook. In an effort to condition his players to the high decibel of crowd noise, which he'd discovered in the compact Silverdome back on that September day, he had rock music blaring over the building's loudspeakers during his squad's workouts. Walsh was leaving nothing to chance. Then he remembered something else. He wasn't upset by it but simply aware of a situation and allowed for it in his preparations. What Walsh was doing was to make Cincinnati cognizant of the fact that he doesn't forget anything.

"Bruce Coslett was with us last year as an assistant in an intern program," Walsh said about the Bengals' special teams coach. "He has much more insight into what we do than we have into what they do. He's very bright and he's their source, I'm afraid. Who would ever think that we worked to prepare him for coaching and we would have him turn up here?"

By the end of the week, all contingencies had been allowed for, except the threat of snow, and that was out of Walsh's control. The game and the game plan now belonged to the quarterbacks. And Walsh knew both quarterbacks well. Montana was a youngster ready to play the biggest game of his career. He seemed unaffected by all the pre-game pressure. Anderson was a veteran who had reached his peak. Walsh knew that a quarterback in his prime is like vintage wine.

"Anderson is bigger, stronger and much more experienced," Walsh remarked. "He is at the peak of his career and in the best health as a pro. He is able to run the ball extremely well and is a great passer. Montana may have the greatest instincts the game has ever seen. He's only in his second year and he'll be at his best five or six years from now. Rolling out, avoiding the rush and still hitting a primary receiver—he's the best I've ever seen at that.

"I expect one or the other team to score four touchdowns. It won't be a bitter defensive struggle with Anderson and Montana on the field. I suspect both teams will be going for the big play. We usually throw the ball more early in the game and then try to run. I think a big win is unlikely. Neither team will come apart after the other one makes a big play. We are very well matched. It is unfortunate somebody has to lose. The Super Bowl tends to overemphasize winning and losing. The loser shouldn't have to hide his head."

San Francisco's chances for a victory improved with the revelation that Ricky Patton would play after missing the Dallas game two weeks before and also that Freddie Solomon, who sprained his knee in a practice accident on Thursday, would also be in the starting lineup. Even before these developments, the Niners were made slight favorites. Ronnie Lott couldn't understand why.

"Cincinnati probably has more talent than we do," Lott claimed. "I'm not just saying that to psyche myself up. I'm saying that because it's true. Just look at all the first round draft picks they have. And they're all starters. I think they'll throw everything at us. For them to come out and be complacent with all of their talent, they'd only be hurting themselves. I think they'll come out and throw the book at us.

"I feel they'll try and go deep against us. I think they'll also try to go short, too. Their tight end will play a big part in the game. He gets open a lot. When you have a tight end who can get open like that, it creates a lot of problems for the defense."

The only problem the 49ers encountered occurred hours before the game. Super Bowl dawned dark and dreary. It was overcast and snow was in everyone's thoughts. Fortunately, no snow materialized, and the plows weren't needed. Nevertheless, San Francisco was victimized by a traffic snarl. The Niners were set to leave their hotel in two busses for the 35-minute journey to the Silverdome. Bus No. 1 left at 1:15 and arrived at the stadium on time. However, bus No. 2, with Walsh and Montana, among others, was bogged down in ramp traffic about a half mile from the Silverdome. What contributed to the tie-up, even though it was still hours before the 4:15 kick-off, was a motorcycle carrying Vice President George Bush. The result was a major traffic jam.

"Coach Walsh was pretty loose on the bus," Montana confided. "He said, 'I've got the radio on and we're leading 7-0. The trainer's calling the plays.' "

Shortly after, Walsh sat staring out the window, thinking of his alternatives. What if traffic conditions remain clogged and the bus can't go any farther?

"After sitting there for 20 minutes, I was starting to get a little uneasy," Walsh admitted. "Everyone was cracking jokes, but I was looking at the angle we'd have to take to walk to the stadium, a cross country trip, each person holding onto the next one's shirt so we wouldn't get blown over."

Walsh's evacuation plan wasn't needed. Finally, at 2:40, bus No. 2 arrived at the players' entrance, only minutes before the 49ers were scheduled to take their warm-ups. It was all in a week's work—the uneasy sleeping hours, the early practice sessions and now this. Walsh had always maintained that his team had character. They were certainly being tested.

If the 49ers had lost the coin toss to determine what time they would practice, their fortunes changed immediately before the game. They won the coin flip and elected to receive the kickoff. It was just what they wanted. What happened after that wasn't. When Jim Breech's kick sailed out of bounds he had to kick over. When he did, Amos Lawrence couldn't hold onto the ball. He fumbled and John Simmons recovered for Cincinnati on the 26 yard line. It certainly wasn't the way the 49ers wanted to begin. A turnover on the very first play had Bengal fans cheering.

Anderson kept them hollering when he hit wide receiver Isaac Curtis with a quick, eight-

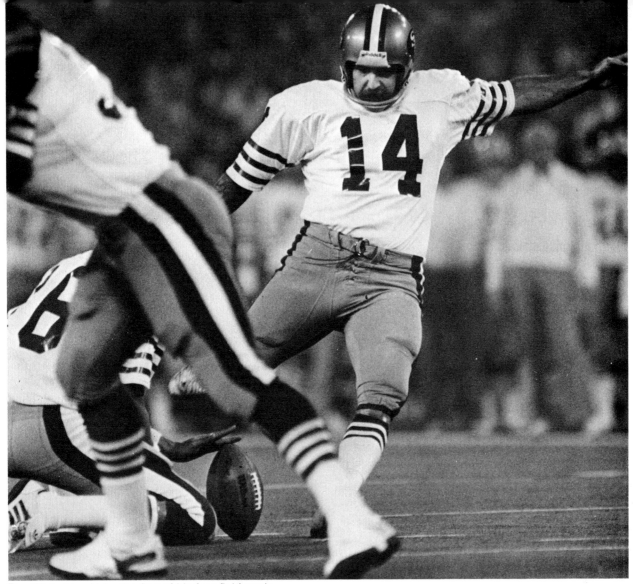

Ray Wersching kicks the first of his four field goals.

yard pass on the 18 yard line. The bull-like Johnson didn't wait long to pick up the game's initial first down by reaching the 16. In just two plays, Cincinnati was already threatening. Anderson created further concern when he connected with tight end Dan Ross for 11 yards to the five. The Bengals were in a superior position to strike. The Niners defense had to repel them. Willie Harper came up fast and stopped Charles Alexander for no gain. Next, Jim Stuckey broke through and sacked Anderson on the 11 yard line. On third down, Anderson looked to throw. He fired toward Curtis on the five yard line but Hicks intercepted and got to the 32 yard line before he was stopped. The Niners were out of trouble. Turning back the Bengals' opening charge with their backs against the wall gave them a lift.

Anticipating a Bengal rush on defense, Montana called a screen pass and completed it to Patton for six yards. He came right back, this time with a six-yard flip to Clark and a first down on the 44 yard line. Earl Cooper couldn't gain anything and Montana went back to the air, completing a nine-yard pass to Solomon. The Niners reached Cincinnati territory but were still a yard short of a first down.

The Bengals braced for the run. It never came. Instead, Patton started to his right and handed off to Solomon in what appeared to be a reverse. However, Solomon lateralled the ball back to Montana, who was calmly poised with what looked like a Chinese fire drill taking place in front of him. Montana lofted a 14-yard pass into the arms of Charle Young for a first down on the 33 yard line that left the Bengals looking at one another in amazement, and the crowd of 81,270 howling with

Eason Ramson high fives Earl Cooper after the big running back scored the 49ers' second touchdown in the second period.

delight.

Montana threw incomplete to tight end Eason Ramson on a pass that was almost intercepted by cornerback Louis Breeden. Then he switched. On a slight delay, he handed the ball to Cooper, who broke through inside right end for 11 yards and a first down on the 22 yard line. Bill Ring came in and immediately became part of the action. He ran the same way Cooper did and picked up seven more yards to the 15. When Cooper tried to go left, he was turned back without a yard. Montana faced his first crucial third down play of the game. He came through. Looking for Solomon, he connected with a 14-yard aerial to the one yard line. The 49ers were knocking on the door.

Montana didn't wait to kick it down. He dove high over center, above a wall of bodies, to score the game's first touchdown. It culminated a smart-looking drive that had covered 68 yards in 11 plays. Wersching easily added the conversion to give the 49ers a 7-0 lead. They had wanted to score first and they did.

Wersching's first kickoff was handled without incident by David Verser. He caught it on the five and returned it to the 19 yard line. Anderson brought the offense on the field for the second time with 5:43 remaining in the

first period. He started with a quick three-yard flip to Johnson. He threw to Johnson again and picked up five more yards. Keeping the ball on a bootleg, Anderson got three yards and a first down on the 30 yard line. The burly Johnson tried inside and gained three yards. Finding no one open on second down, Anderson kept the ball and ran for six yards around left end. Johnson then supplied the necessary first down yardage when he got to the 41.

Anderson then tried to catch the Niners napping by going deep. However, his long pass to wide receiver Cris Collinsworth was defended flawlessly by Eric Wright. Again Anderson went to Collinsworth and missed for the second time. On third down, Keena Turner didn't give Anderson a chance to throw. He nailed him for a four-yard loss that forced the Bengals to punt. Pat McInally came through with a strong kick that left the 49ers in weak field position when the ball was downed on the 10 yard line.

With 1:01 left, Montana tried a quick flare pass to Clark that was broken up by cornerback Ken Riley. Cincinnati defensive end Ross Browner placed the Niners in a precarious situation when he dropped Patton for a seven-yard loss on the three yard line. They got a bit of relief before the next play when the Bengals were penalized for having 12 men on the field. Still, Patton could only run for four yards to the 12 on the last play of the quarter.

Jim Miller had to punt from the end zone when the second period action began. He delivered a 44-yard punt that gave Cincinnati choice field position just one yard short of midfield. Johnson ran to the right for the third straight time and gained five yards. Anderson saw something and called time out. He conferred with Gregg, came back to take the snap and completed an 18-yard pass to Collinsworth on the San Francisco 28. A five-yard false start penalty set them back to the 33. Anderson just missed on a pass to Ross as an official ruled that the ball was trapped. An illegal contact cost the 49ers a five-yard penalty and a first down on the 28 yard line. After Alexander could only get a yard, Anderson brought the crowd to its feet. He completed a 19-yard pass to Collinsworth on the eight-yard line.

With time running out in the final period, Wersching kicks his third field goal.

However, Wright stripped the ball from the rookie wide receiver and Lynn Thomas recovered it.

For the second straight time, the Niners were in a risky end of the field. They had to play it safe. Johnny Davis got a yard and then Ring added two more to the 11. Montana had to come up with a big third down play. He did. Rolling to his right, he stopped long enough to direct a 20-yard pass to Solomon on the 31 yard line. The completion not only got the 49ers out of danger, but produced a key first down.

Montana called the same pass route. However, finding no one open, he scrambled for eight yards before he was brought down on the 39. Cooper then found an opening around right end and churned for 14 yards to the Cincinnati 47 yard line. Patton kept it going with a four-yard advance. However, when Montana missed with a pass to Solomon, he faced another key third down play. He came through again. This time he turned to Clark and connected on a 12-yard pass.

The 49ers had a solid drive working. It had begun on their eight yard line, and now they were standing on the Cincinnati 31. They kept moving. On a quick trap, Patton burst up the middle for nine yards. He got the first down on his next carry when he reached the 19 yard line. It appeared that Clark had lost two yards when the 49ers tried an end around on the very next play. But in stopping the play, Ben-gal linebacker Jim LeClair committed a personal foul and was assessed a 10-yard penalty.

With the ball now on the 11 yard line, Montana went for the quick kill. He sent his receivers out and deftly tossed a pass to Cooper coming out of the backfield. The big fullback found an open area on the three yard line and continued into the end zone standing up for the Niners' second touchdown. The 92-yard drive, the longest in Super Bowl history, was completed in 12 plays. Wersching's conversion sent San Francisco into a 14-0 lead.

Now one of Walsh's ideas paid off. Verser had difficulty controlling Wersching's squib kick and was tackled at the four yard line. An illegal chuck on the kickoff penalized Cincinnati half the distance to the goal line, which meant that Anderson had to get the Bengals out of trouble starting from the two yard line. After Johnson cracked over center for four yards, Anderson threw a 10-yard pass to Ross for a first down on the 16. Since it was successful, the veteran quarterback decided to keep passing. However, he failed to complete his next two passes. His third one to Ross gained only nine yards and left Cincinnati a yard short of a first down. McInally had to punt from the 25, and he sent a 44-yard kick to Hicks, who ran it back six yards to the San Francisco 34.

There was 4:11 remaining in the first half and Montana was still thinking about putting more points on the board. He started on his

179

Jim Miller gets off a pressure punt from the end zone.

way with a 17-yard pass to Clark on the Cincinnati 49 yard line. Changing his attack, he turned to Patton. He got three yards on his first carry but then shook loose for seven more the second time he ran and a first down on the 39 yard line. Just before the two-minute warning, Montana flipped a short four-yard pass to Cooper on the 35.

Only 1:57 remained when play was resumed. On first down, Montana threw incomplete to Young. He then looked for Clark and found him for a first down on the 25 yard line. Montana switched to the run. Patton got three yards and Cooper got six as the Niners reached the 16 yard line. There were 54 seconds left when San Francisco called for time. Montana and Walsh conferred on the sidelines. It was decided that Montana would sneak for the first down and then without huddling throw a pass to Solomon on the next play.

Time was now a factor. Montana moved for two yards and a first down on the 14 yard line. The pass to Solomon worked for nine yards to the five. San Francisco fans were cheering for another touchdown. Operating quickly, Montana tried to get it with Clark but the pass was

knocked down. He tried still another pass that sailed out of the end zone. With just 18 seconds left on the clock, Wersching produced a 22-yard field goal that built the 49ers' lead to 17-0.

Although there were only 15 seconds showing on the clock, the Niners weren't done. Wersching's deliberate squib kick was fumbled by Archie Griffin on the 15 yard line. The loose ball rolled toward the Bengal goal line and a resourceful Milt McColl recovered it for the 49ers on the four. The Bengals were stunned. San Francisco was primed to score again. Wersching never left the field. With five seconds left in the half, there was only time for a field goal. An illegal procedure infraction positioned the ball on the nine yard line. Wersching took it from there. He drilled a 26-yard field goal that extended San Francisco's advantage to 20-0. They had jumped on top just the way they'd hoped.

The Bengals' frustration was evident when Wersching kicked off with only two seconds left. Guy Frazier was content with merely covering the ball on the 28 yard line. He fell on Wersching's squibber, making certain that the ball would not get away again. The squib kicks that Wersching had practiced all week on the hard surface of the Silverdome worked to perfection. The Bengals seemed to be in shock.

San Francisco had totally dominated the first half as the teams went into the dressing rooms to the cheers of their faithful fans. It showed in the statistics, too. They gained 208 yards to Cincinnati's 99, had 38 plays to 25, and produced 15 first downs to seven. Individually, Montana was outplaying Anderson. He completed 12 of 18 passes for 132 yards and a touchdown, while Anderson was eight of 14 for only 83 yards. The 49ers were halfway to the first world championship in San Francisco history.

If the Bengals were to get back into the game and prevent a blowout, it was imperative that they score immediately after the second-half kickoff. This time, Verser handled Wersching's kick cleanly on the one yard line, and returned it 16 yards to the 17. It was up to Anderson to ignite the Bengal offense.

Alexander found some daylight around right end and moved for 13 yards and a first down. A face mask penalty on Hicks added five more yards on the play and advanced the ball to the 35. Johnson ran the same direction Alexander did but was halted after he got three yards. Anderson tried to break Alexander open with a short pass in the right flat, but Williamson held him to a gain of only three yards. Anderson now faced a third and four on his 41. He had to keep the drive going. He did. He hooked up with Steve Kreider on a well-timed, 19-yard pass on the San Francisco 40.

On a quick opener, Johnson bolted over right guard for five yards. Then the Bengals pulled something out of the 49ers' playbook. Anderson handed the ball to Griffin, who started running to his right. He stopped and lateralled the ball back to Anderson. Looking downfield, Anderson threw a 13-yard pass to Curtis on the 22. There was more. The Niners were flagged for a face mask penalty on the play, which brought the ball to the 11 yard line. The Bengals were growling now. On first down, Griffin gained four yards, then Johnson was stopped after he picked up two. On third down from the five yard line, Anderson faded back to pass. He looked to his left, then his right. Even the middle was jammed. He decided it would be wiser to run and made it to the end zone for Cincinnati's first touchdown. The 83-yard drive had consumed only 3:35 in nine plays. Jim Breech's conversion reduced San Francisco's lead to 20-7.

One could feel the momentum changing when Montana started out on the 20 yard line after Breech's kickoff sailed through the end zone. It began when Browner broke through and sacked Montana on the 11. Montana's second down pass to Solomon was knocked away by Breeden. When Patton could only circle right end for four yards, the Niners had to punt. Miller got off a 47-yarder to Mike Fuller on the Bengal 38. Running to his right, Fuller made a neat 13-yard return to the San Francisco 49. The Bengals had choice field position. Still trying to break loose, Johnson was contained after he got three yards. Anderson went to the pass, but threw too low for Collinsworth. On third down, he tried again. He was flushed out of the pocket by a strong rush and Leopold chased him out of bounds with-

out yielding a yard.

San Francisco went back on the attack after Solomon signaled for a fair catch of McInally's punt on the 15 yard line. Once again, the Niners had negative field position. Cooper tried to go wide but was nailed for a two-yard loss by linebacker Jim LeClair. On second down, Ring could only gain a yard. Not taking any chances, Montana flipped a short, high-percentage pass to Ring which resulted in just a three-yard advance. The 49ers had to punt; even more depressing was the fact that in six plays, midway through the third period, they were stifled for minus three yards.

Miller delivered a pressure 50-yard punt to the Cincinnati 33 yard line. The opportunistic Fuller made another fine runback, this time getting 17 yards to midfield. The Bengals were in excellent field location to strike again. They lost some of the advantage with a holding penalty on the first down that set them back to their own 41 yard line. Again, on second down, the Bengals were victimized by a

Walt Easley looks to get by Cincinnati defensive end Ross Browner.

Dwaine Board breaks through.

penalty. A 15-yard pass completion to Ross was negated by a personal foul infraction. Anderson now was confronted with a second and 19 predicament. Dean added to his dilemma on the very next play by sacking Anderson with a four yard loss. Maybe, now, the momentum was swinging back.

Anderson grimly discussed a third and 23 situation in the huddle. They were now on their 37 yard line after beginning at midfield. Anderson set three receivers to his left and dropped back to throw. He got good protection as he unleashed a long, high, arching pass to Collinsworth down the left sideline. The speedy receiver, immersed in concentration,

looked over his right shoulder, reached up and gathered in the ball over Wright's outstretched arms. He was tackled immediately on the 14 yard line, following a picture-book 49-yard gain. The big play injected new life into the Bengals.

Cincinnati entertained visions of scoring. Reynolds was determined to stop them. On first down he knocked Alexander down after he gained a yard. Anderson got his next pass off, and completed it to Ross on the five yard line. Still, the Bengals were a yard short of a first down. Should they go for it or settle for a field goal that would reduce San Francisco's once 20-0 margin to 20-10?

They decided to go for it. Johnson bulled his way for two yards and the first down before he was stopped by Board on the three yard line. The Bengals now had four tries at getting the three yards needed for a touchdown. Johnson and Alexander were tough short yardage runners. It didn't appear possible they could be denied, except perhaps for a fumble. That's what Niner fans were hoping for as the San Francisco defense dug in for the expected charge by Johnson or Alexander.

Johnson tried the middle and banged his way forward for two yards. Now they had three downs to get only a single yard. The 49ers employed six linemen and four linebackers with only Ronnie Lott in the secondary. Johnson tried to get the yard over left guard, the Bengals' bread-and-butter play in which the monster fullback follows a lead block by Alexander into a hole produced by the Bengals' two best linemen, Munoz and guard Dave Lapham. It couldn't miss, except that reserve linebacker Dan Bunz isn't one to be convinced. He jammed Alexander into the hole which enabled reserve tackle John Harty to grab Johnson low while Reynolds banged him high

for no gain.

Anderson and the Bengals were astonished. Johnson is regarded as unstoppable on that play, and yet the Niners repulsed him. On third down, Anderson felt more comfortable going to a pass. He called for a short one to Alexander, one in which Anderson rolls to his right and dumps a little dinky pass into Alexander's arms. He completed it but never figured that Bunz would be keying on Alexander. The determined Bunz decked Alexander with a jarring tackle the moment he caught the ball. No gain!

The San Francisco fans sitting in that part of the end zone were in a frenzy. The Bengals went back into their huddle with looks of bewilderment. Their two primary plays in a goal line situation had been dismembered. Anderson decided it was prudent to call a time out. He wanted to be certain of the final play. The decision was to give it to Johnson, this time to the right of center running behind Alexander. Bunz wasn't buying it. He stuffed Alexander, the same way he'd done two plays earlier, and slowed down Johnson's charge long enough for half of the 49er line, led by the reckless Reynolds, to stop him. The Silverdome went

Owner Ed DeBartolo, Jr. accepts the Vince Lombardi Trophy from Commissioner Pete Rozelle at far left. CBS announcer Brent Mussberger congratulates DeBartolo as coach Bill Walsh and linebackers Jack Reynolds and Dan Bunz look on.

Montana clutches the game-winning ball as he makes his way through a group of photographers.

wild. It was the most dramatic goal line stand in the 16-year history of the Super Bowl.

The clock showed only 1:17 remaining in the third period when the 49er offense took over on the one yard line. It certainly wasn't an enviable position, but they were buoyant after the remarkable performance by the defense in denying the Bengals a certain touchdown. Montana was limited in his play selection with the goal posts at his back; he had to play it close. He gave the ball to Ring twice, who gained three yards and then four yards before time elapsed in the third period. The 49ers were still ahead, 20-7.

On the first play of the fourth quarter, Cooper's draw play resulted in only a one-yard gain, leaving the 49ers two yards short of a first down. It meant that Miller had to punt under pressure again from the nine yard line. Braced for the snap in the end zone, Miller got off a 44-yard kick to the Cincinnati 47 yard line. This time the pesky Fuller was hit immediately by Randy Cross.

For the third consecutive time, the Bengals had advantageous field position. Johnson got them to midfield with a three-yard thrust. It was at this point that Anderson decided it was time to start passing again. He hit Collinsworth on a crossing pattern in the middle for 12 yards. Then he went to Ross on a slant

Montana and Earl Cooper share a laugh with Mussberger.

in the same section for nine more yards. Suddenly, the Bengals were on the Niner 29 needing only a yard for a first down.

They got much more. Lott was called for pass interference, which presented Cincinnati with a first down on the 15 yard line. The Bengals were back applying scoring pressure. After throwing low on first down, Anderson completed a nine-yard pass to Ross on the six yard line. The Bengals got closer when Alexander dove over center for two yards for a first down on the four. This time, the Bengals didn't wait for any further goal line dramatics by the 49ers. Anderson tossed a four-yard touchdown strike to Ross. Breech's conversion cut San Francisco's comfortable 20-0 lead to a tenuous 20-14.

It was imperative that Montana generate some momentum. The kickoff positioned the ball on the 27 yard line—something of a luxury for the young quarterback. The previous three times he had had the ball in the third period weren't exactly choice spots from which to mount an offense. He was determined to get more points on the board. If he didn't Cincinnati was only a touchdown away from taking over the lead.

San Francisco didn't start out too solidly. Montana's first pass was deflected by linebacker Reggie Williams. On second down, Dan Audick made a false start which cost the Niners five yards. Montana was now challenged by a second and 15 call. He had to pass. He took the snap and rolled to his right. He looked for reserve receiver Mike Wilson near the sidelines. Wilson ran upfield then came back toward Montana, who delivered the ball perfectly into his hands. The 22-yard completion provided the 49ers with a big first down on the 44 yard line, pulling them away from the shadow of their goal line.

The play seemed to give the Niners the lift they needed. A pass interference penalty on Bengal cornerback Ken Riley gave San Francisco a first down on the 49. Patton broke loose from there for ten yards to the Cincinnati 41 yard line. Patton tried it again and got two yards. When he ran for the third straight time, he collected seven yards to the Bengals' 32 yard line. On third and one, Montana picked

185

up the first down himself by sneaking inside right tackle for four yards.

With the football resting on the 28 yard line, the 49ers were on the perimeter of field goal distance. A field goal at this point in the game would almost be the equivalent of a touchdown, since it would stretch San Francisco's lead to nine points. Cooper ran for a yard. Patton added three more yards and still another on his final carry to reach the 23. It was time for Wersching to enter the game for an important field goal. He lined up a 40-yard attempt with Montana pointing to where Wersching wanted the quarterback to spot the ball. His kick was strong and accurate. It easily cleared the crossbar to stretch the 49ers' margin to 23-14.

Time was San Francisco's ally now. There was only 5:14 on the clock when the Bengals started on offense, following the kickoff. Verser's eight-yard return on Wersching's kick put the ball on the 22 yard line. All Anderson could do now was to pass. The Niner defense was alerted to it, too. On Anderson's first pass attempt to Collinsworth, Wright swooped in and plucked the ball off on the Cincinnati 47 yard line. Wright had hopes of running back the interception for a touchdown. He got down to the 22 yard line before being hit from behind by guard Max Montoya and fumbling. However, Willie Harper, who was trailing the play, pounced on the ball and recovered it for the Niners.

San Francisco was already in field goal range. Obviously that was their thinking as Patton ran right for four yards. Cooper went the same way for three more. On third down, Johnnny Davis went the other way for four yards and a first down on the 10 yard line. The 49ers were that much closer. Patton ran right again to collect four more yards. But when he tried it again, he was dropped for a six-yard loss back on the 13 yard line. It didn't matter. On the next play, Montana kept the ball and bootlegged it around left end for seven yards to the six. There were only two minutes left when Wersching entered the game to try a 23-yard field goal. He came through again to seal the 49ers' place in history, 26-14.

Officially, there was 1:51 remaining when Cincinnati began its final drive on their 26 yard line. There wasn't really any way they could overcome San Francisco's lead in that period of time, no matter how many passes Anderson threw. He started with a 21-yard completion to Curtis and then a 16-yard one to Ross. From the San Francisco 37 yard line, he passed to Ross for eight more yards and to Collinsworth for nine and a first down on the 20. Anderson was left with 25 seconds. He kept throwing to complete a 17-yard pass to Kreider on the three yard line. Going without a huddle, he fired a quick three-yard pass to Ross for a touchdown. It was all anticlimatic. Breech's conversion only upped the final score to 26-21.

The one possible remaining danger to the 49ers would be their failure to cover an onside kickoff. Walsh prepared for it by employing his sure-handed receivers when the Niners lined up to accept Breech's abbreviated kick. Breech topped the ball in the direction of Clark who performed what was expected of him by catching the ball and falling down to secure possession. Clark, who had clinched the Dallas victory, now guaranteed the Super Bowl triumph. The last play of the game was routine. Montana took the snap and fell down as time expired. The Niners were ready to celebrate their finest hour. It had taken 36 years.

Perhaps they had expected to win, just the way they had done all season long. It was Walsh's contention to approach this game as if it were just another in a long campaign. His calming effect worked almost too well.

On Thursday night, the players had called a meeting without any coaches, to redefine what they were there for. Their practices up until that time had not been sharp; they were, to some degree, lethargic. Realizing their ineptitude, the players wanted to stress the importance of concentrating more on what was expected of them. The meeting proved effective. The players had a satisfactory workout on Friday, which carried over into the final one on Saturday.

"We could see that it was needed because we were losing our concentration in practice," Fahnhorst said. "A lot of guys were missing assignments and that type of thing. It was get-

Dwight Clark acknowledges the San Francisco fans.

ting a little too close to game time. I think some guys had to be reminded how important things were. I think it really helped because the next day we had a great practice."

"I was kind of scared this morning thinking about the game," Cross confessed in the crowded dressing room after the victory. "We practiced this week with rock music blaring on the field. Guys were on the field picking 'air guitars.' Even in the team meeting everyone seemed so relaxed. I wondered because this was the Super Bowl. Before the game in the dressing room, Coach Bill Walsh played, 'This Is It,' by Kenny Loggins. The song had a message. You have a once-in-a-lifetime chance and as the quote in the song goes '. . . this is your miracle.' You have to grab it.

"It was Montana's idea to play it. After we'd played it once, everybody said, 'Let's get seri-ous and think about the game,' and Bill's over there saying, 'Where is the music? Play that song again.'"

It was in sharp contrast to the legendary Notre Dame coach Knute Rockne's way of preparing his teams for a big game. In one dressing room scene, he exhorted his players to, '. . . win one for the Gipper,' an Irish player named George Gipp who had died and was portrayed in the movie by actor Ronald Reagan. Only now, actor-turned-President Reagan had called Walsh shortly after the game to offer his congratulations.

"Hello, Coach Walsh, this is Ronald Reagan."

"I thought it might be."

"I just wanted to tell you a couple of Californians want to congratulate you and the entire team. And you might tell Joe Montana and the fellas that they really did win one for the Gipper."

"I think Joe was thinking of the Gipper when he won. Thank you very much. I enjoyed shaking your hand the other night and I was hoping I would receive a call from you in about two weeks. I'll tell Joe about the Gipper. Thank you very, very much."

Walsh received congratulations from a number of notables who gained access to the dressing room. The well-wishers included Governor Jerry Brown and such 49er luminaries as O.J. Simpson, Frankie Albert and Bob St. Clair. It was Walsh's finest hour, and he deserved the accolades.

"This is the greatest moment of my life," he said. "This is the ultimate goal of my career. I cannot conceive of a more satisfying moment to have taken a team and in three years develop it into a Super Bowl champion. We brought the world championship to a great city. It is a rare moment for me to work with such a great group of men and win a championship. This is a group of men who have great talent, and great inspiration. No one could take us this year. This is the highlight of my life. Anything can happen now.

"In the beginning it was 50 against the world. Sometimes we had problems convincing everyone, even those in our own area. Many NFL personnel directors picked Cincinnati, because all they had to do was get out their computer printout sheets; but the NFL players picked us because of our chemistry. And chemistry is what wins."

Then Walsh stopped for a moment to talk about some of the key plays in the game that contributed to the triumph.

"If I had to pick key plays, I would say one was the pass we completed to Mike Wilson in the fourth quarter," Walsh said. "The second was the interception by Eric Wright when we were leading, 23-14, in the last quarter that led to Ray Wersching's fourth field goal.

"The goal line stand is something we have done before. That is where we showed our character, when you won't give up on the one-foot line. Bunz and Reynolds were tremendous. That might have been the difference in the ball game. I would also say the turning point was the field goal in the last five seconds of the first half.

"Basically our offense swept them off their feet in the first half and then we had to depend on the defense to hold the fort when they came out charging in the second half. At halftime, I told the team what to expect. We knew we were playing a great football team. Maybe, if the score was 24-0 they might have caved in, but not with only 20-0. We did have to abandon our game plan for part of the second half. We were in a hole most of the time. If we ever got the ball in good position, we could have opened up more. We finally got untracked in the fourth quarter."

Montana was as calm after the game as he was on the field. He leaned back sipping a can of soda, talking to a horde of media people.

"The feeling of winning this game hasn't really sunk in yet," Montana said. "I have a lot of emotion about it right now, but I don't think that it will hit me until after I get showered and dressed. People didn't believe we would make the playoffs. Even when we started winning the big games, people still didn't believe in us. I mean people around the country.

"We beat Dallas and nobody believed in us. We beat Pittsburgh. We beat Cincinnati in Cincinnati. And they still didn't believe in us. Dallas, a second time in the championship game and people still didn't believe. Even the coaches around the league. Most of them picked against us in the Super Bowl. People didn't start to believe in us until, oh, say, about two minutes ago."

San Francisco	7	13	0	6	26
Cincinnati	0	0	7	14	21

San Francisco: 9:08, first period—Montana 1 yard run (Wersching, kick)
San Francisco: 8:07, second period—Cooper 11 yard pass from Montana (Wersching, kick)
San Francisco: 14:45, second period—22 yard field goal, Wersching
San Francisco: 14:58, second period—26 yard field goal, Wersching
Cincinnati: 3:35, third period—Anderson 5 yard run (Breech, kick)
Cincinnati: 4:54, fourth period—Ross 4 yard pass from Anderson (Breech, kick)
San Francisco: 9:35, fourth period—40 yard field goa, Wersching
San Francisco: 13:03, fourth period—23 yard field goal, Wersching
Cincinnati: 14:44, fourth period—Ross 3 yard pass from Anderson (Breech, kick)